DUST TO DEW

BETTY
IRABOR

Published in Nigeria in 2018 by Quramo Publishing
under its QLife imprint

The Simi Johnson Centre
13, Sinari Daranijo Street, Victoria Island
Lagos, Nigeria.
+234 01 454 7878
info@quramo.com
www.quramo.com

A catalogue record of this book will be available from the National Library of
Nigeria.

ISBN: 978-978-965-742-1

DUST TO DEW

BETTY IRABOR

DEDICATION

To the sweet memory of Fred Belo-Osagie.

CONTENTS

FOREWORD

As a child, I was prone to melancholy.

When the feeling came over me, it was one of profound sadness and worthlessness. I could feel it descending and yet there was nothing I could do about it. It took a while before I could even put a name to these emotions.

My first memory of this melancholy registered as an 'out of sorts' kind of feeling. I couldn't put a name to what it was but it didn't feel good. I was visiting an aunt who doted on me, as I was named after her. I was around seven at the time. I felt awful and I was bewildered; I didn't understand this horrible feeling and so I started to cry.

In hindsight, I realise this was my first conscious brush with depression. I have had mild and serious bouts of it all my life. I am lucky, I am in a place where I have coping mechanisms for dealing with it. This significant part of my life is a secret from majority of people, apart from a few very close friends. The stigma, the sniggers, and the dangers of ostracism that follow any indication of mental health problems, ensured that I didn't share this part of my life easily. Now it has found its way into this book thanks to the courage of Betty Irabor, its author.

In *Dust to Dew*, Betty takes us through her traumatic and painful battle with depression. She agonisingly unpacks this debilitating disease, and in doing so shines a light on the darkness it typifies. We see, first hand, through the eyes of a sufferer, the devastating nature of depression, an illness that is mostly shrouded in secrecy amid stigma and shame.

Yet this illness is more common than people care to admit. According to a World Bank report released last month, twenty-two percent of Nigerians suffer from chronic depression. If we take a conservative estimate of our population at one-fifty million people, it means some thirty-three million are affected. If this was Polio, Tuberculosis or any type of physical illness affecting the populace in such numbers, everybody would be talking about it. There would be loud demands for treatment centres, and maybe even calls for the declaration of a national emergency to deal with the problem. International donors would rush to get involved in finding solutions.

Not so for depression. We do not have the requisite skills and facilities for treating depression, we don't talk about it; we actually do our best to hide it. Our culture, if truth be told, equates pretty much every mental illness with madness. So we deny, pretend, sidestep, obfuscate, hide and do anything that stops us from coming to grips with the problem. The unfortunate result is that millions suffer in silence, and often with dire consequences.

Dust to Dew is therefore a momentous work, particularly because it has been written by an iconic figure in Nigeria. To the majority of Nigerians, Betty Irabor has it all. We see her adorning the fashion pages of our newspapers and magazines, her svelte figure encased in beautiful gowns, throat and ears adorned with exquisite jewellery, often with her husband at her side, an epitome of success in all its ramifications.

Betty is the publisher of one of the successful magazines in Nigeria, mother to a young man and young woman, who are doing well in their own right; wife to a successful man. Her life is 'picture perfect' and the envy of many.

Except it isn't perfect – she has been in a life and death struggle with depression.

The thing with this illness is that it has no regard for reality, as we see through Betty's experience. So although she is extremely successful by most measurable standards in life, her success didn't matter. The depression insisted she was worthless, and she believed it. The illness consumed her to such an extent that everything she had been and was, disappeared. She simply didn't see it. The people around her who cared deeply about her - her children, her sisters, her husband - kept trying to remind her with reality and truth but it didn't register and she just couldn't believe them.

This is what depression does.

The illness is clinically defined as a serious mood disorder which affects how we feel, think, and act, and causes feelings of sadness and can affect our interest in life and everyday activities. As you'll see in Betty's account that follows, it is also not a respecter of persons.

As I am writing this in Lagos, I am also mourning the untimely death by suicide of a colleague in the profession whose public profile also cut the image of someone who has it all. I speak of Anthony Bourdain, celebrity chef, beloved by everyone who interacted with him through his show, "Parts Unknown".

From millions who only knew him on screen from a distance, to those like US President Barack Obama and I, who were lucky enough to have featured at different times on his show and shared a meal with him, the conclusion about Bourdain was the same.

This was a man who cared deeply about the people whose lives he tried to understand, and whose cultures he tried to share and illuminate, through their cuisine. This empathy and authenticity gave him a critically acclaimed, international award-winning show, a measure of financial success, an opportunity to travel the world and millions of fans. With a daughter whom he doted on, he 'had it all', but in the end, it wasn't enough to keep him here, and his millions of admirers have been left wondering what happened.

We are lucky therefore to have Betty's personal account of dealing with depression. To those who haven't dealt with the illness, it will give insight into what the darkness looks like, and hopefully guide them so they know how to spot and help those who are suffering. For the millions of us who have experienced it, hopefully Betty's courage will rub off on us and we will finally be brave enough to not just share our own stories, but also seek the help that we need. This book should also be a wakeup call to the medical profession in Nigeria to begin to focus on nurturing the skills and implementing the facilities needed for the effective treatment of depression and other mental illness.

I am particularly honoured that Betty trusted me with the task of writing this foreword. We owe her a debt of gratitude. By lifting the veil on depression, by shining a bright light into its dark enveloping clouds, explaining it, detailing her journey to recovery, she is contributing in no small way to the fight against this disease and other types of mental illness, and will probably save many lives. I urge you to read this book with an open mind and when you finish reading it, hand it over to a friend.

You never know... you may be saving a life.

Kadaria Ahmed
June 2018
Lagos

PREFACE

Dust is chaos.

When I conceived the title of this book, I went back in time to my childhood, a harrowing day in the barracks I grew up in. I thought about how it felt to watch my father leave, trying to wave at him as the car zoomed off, raising a huge cloud of dust that left specks in my eyes. The idea for **Dust to Dew** was born. Dust blinds. It inhibits joy, clouds visibility, arrests creativity, and stunts growth.

Why dew?

Because it soothes, and when the dust of our lives settles, we can see episodes from our past from a more refreshing perspective; the gloom lifts and we're able to channel our suppressed emotion into breathing ideas. Dew *calms* Dust.

Over the years, as I have honed my personal philosophies, I have come to realise how important a positive emotional energy is. Dew represents that positivity, that clarity. My goal is to be happy, and life has taught me that happiness is a gift you give yourself; no one has a monopoly over it. The path to that happiness begins with believing that you deserve it, that you are worthy of a joyful existence. I hope this book encourages you to open up, to find healing and closure. I hope it leads you to understand that bad things happen to the best of us, and that we don't have to have it all figured out at once.

Dew brings hope; it is hope renewed. A dew drop speaks to me of a fresh start. After everything I have been through, I can now look at my achievements with pride, knowing that I have fought the good fight and I am well on course to finishing the race strong. *Genevieve Magazine* is a product of many sacrifices. I have been privileged to watch the transformation of the brand to world class status. It is an achievement that gladdens my heart. I am the proud author of 'Morning Dew,' and this new work, both great testimonies to my life's journey. I have mentored so many people from different walks of life and spoken at reputable national and international events on diverse subjects, winning numerous awards along the way. I have had huge successes for which I am grateful. I used to despise the process, but it has become for me the inspiration for the stories I have to tell; the story of a near-chequered childhood and a beautiful adulthood that was temporarily blighted by depression.

Depression is like being trapped between elevator floors. When the elevator finally opens for you to escape, you're too afraid to step out into the real world. You have the keys to the door, but you're afraid to unlock it because you're trapped by your fears. You're in quicksand, waiting to be swallowed into eternal darkness. You're numb and the only thing you can feel is grief. You may feel lost, like you have missed your way and you cannot be saved. In the depth of despair, it might help to draw strength from the message of one of my favourite parables, The Parable of the Lost Sheep. Even if you feel right now like the lost sheep, remember that God is coming right out to look for you.

I want you to be unstoppable in the pursuit of your own joy. It may not seem like it now, but today will be tomorrow's inspiration. Dew gives new life. You must allow yourself to go through the transition from the years of dust in order to come to the years of dew.

Betty
May 2018
Lagos

PROLOGUE

I heard the voice again, *you're no good*. I tried to ignore it but it wouldn't go unheard. *You are nothing; you are just a big fat failure!*

The hand of trauma is long and strong, stretching over decades and slowly choking out life, as it demands to be dealt with.

With those words ricocheting around my head, I climbed back into bed and slid the duvet over my head. I could still hear it, so I got up and adjusted the curtains until I could not see a glimmer of light. I felt my way along the walls and back to my bed, where I pulled the duvet over my head again. At last, the darkness that enveloped the room matched my world. I hummed Nicole C. Mullen's 'Redeemer' as tears streamed down my cheeks...

> *'The very same God*
> *That spins things in orbit*
> *He runs to the weary,*
> *The worn and the weak*
> *And the same gentle hands*
> *That hold me when I'm broken*
> *They conquered death to bring me victory*
> *Now I know my Redeemer lives...'*

I don't know for how long I was curled up crying and humming in the dark before my phone rang. Even before I checked the caller ID, I knew it was Barbara, my best friend. She had been calling me for days, but I always did the same thing—I let the sound ring out. This time, once the ringing stopped, I switched off the phone.

I longed for sleep, but in spite of the pitch darkness, it remained elusive as it had for months. Even though I had been prescribed many strong sedatives and antidepressants, it seemed minutes blended into hours and days into nights. Months came and went yet my body would just not go to sleep. My thoughts screamed in my head in the quiet evening, and all I could hear was the same taunting voice that told me I was no good. When it first started, I had tried to remind myself of all my accomplishments. *I am Betty, Publisher of the foremost lifestyle magazine in Nigeria; The lady who started the advocacy for breast cancer awareness in Nigeria, with the Pink Ball; Everyone's favourite aunty, who inspires; Madam 'Motivator' herself; the forever-young Betty. I've achieved a lot!* I would recount my achievements under my breath to steady myself. However, as the days went by and I remained steeped in my fatigue and bleary-eyed daze, the voice had become louder as it told me: *You are not enough. In spite of all the prescriptions the doctors have given you, you are not better. You're not enough then. Take all these pills at once.*

It seemed everywhere I looked all I saw were clouds. I couldn't see a single flicker of light on the horizon. Everything—my surroundings, my body, the voice, my thoughts, everything—made me feel like I was in the deep end of a pool, and each time I tried to come up for air, something invisible held me down. Each day felt as if I was drowning afresh, and I soon found that it was easier for me to give in than to fight. That was how I came to spend days on end under the duvet in the dark. At least it mirrored what was going on inside me.

How did I get here? I was the woman who, at forty-six, left her comfortable job with a great income to venture into an industry she was repeatedly told was a 'boys club.' How did I go from that woman to being a shell, drowning in the voice of self-doubt and dismay? When I started *Genevieve*, I had been so bold and determined to quiet the naysayers. In spite of the challenges of starting the magazine with a low budget in an informal industry, all my fears at the time had been rational and they had not held me back for even a second. Under the duvet, I no longer cared about the magazine or anything.

I wanted to sleep or slip into non-existence, but my life seemed to flash before me repeatedly, taunting me with better times, like when I was a child and it seemed I could sleep through a storm. Growing up, one of my mum's favourite stories was about how, when I was ten years old, she came back from work on a day I was home alone and fast asleep. She knocked and yelled my name for so long that she had to get the neighbours to help. They took a ladder and climbed up to our window to see me fast asleep on my mat, so they had to pour water on me through the window to wake me.

As an adult, I had somehow lost this ability I hadn't even known was valuable.

3

My fiftieth birthday hadn't been so long ago for me to have forgotten how happy I felt that day. I had a near perfect life – doting husband, lovely children, a close knit family I cherished, a thriving business, great friends, and a lifestyle that I loved. It was one of the most joyous moments of my life, but that peak seemed to be matched in intensity by the darkness I plunged into just two years after.

Clutching the duvet and shaking from the sobs that wracked my frail body, I asked myself again, "How did I get here?"

DUST

CHAPTER 1
THE WORLD KNOWS MY NAME

From the moment I was on my knees, shoulders raised and slightly hunched, leaning forward and waiting for the gun, I would anticipate the speed. I was fast. Sometimes, I felt faster than the breeze because, when I was on the tracks, even the wind was behind me. I loved the sound of the crowd yelling for Betty Belo-Osagie, and the moments when the loud speaker would boom, "Lane three, Betty Belo-Osagie!"

I would smile, thinking, *whoa, the world knows my name. That's my name resounding from the stadium speakers.*

Once the gun went off, I'd just go, go, go, scaling the hurdles. On the tartan track, I would feel the adrenaline, as though something was pumping up my energy. Whether I won the race or not, I would still feel like a winner, and so, for some years, the track was my favourite place as a young girl. It was where my long, skinny k-legs were a plus, not something for me to be self-conscious about. I loved running. I loved the tracks and the feeling was mutual.

At first I had tried sprinting for my school house, Nightingale, but I could not handle it. I had started running on the hurdles team after my Physical Education teacher took interest in me and encouraged me to take up hurdles as a sport.

"You have long legs and you are very agile, you should try hurdles," she insisted.

For a few years before I started running, I had not felt like I was good at anything worthy of being paid attention. In the years following my father's absence, I had become shy and withdrawn in my classes, rarely speaking out of fear that I would say or do something wrong. However, on the tartan track, I had none of those worries. I was my own queen there, win or lose.

"Faster. Faster!"
"Betty!"
"You can do it."

I could hear the chants, and I had only three more hurdles to scale before the finish line. I was in the lead although I was fast losing stamina. As the cheers urged me on, I finally breasted the tape and felt my heart leap in joy and relief. This race was huge. It was different—defining. I had won a ticket to the finals of the national competition. As soon as I crossed that tape, I was on my way to Jos, Nigeria, for the main competition. At the time, I had no inkling that Jos would change what I thought was the set course of my life, so I ran excitedly into the extended arms of my coach as the loudspeaker boomed: "The winner of the 100 metres hurdle heat is Betty Belo-Osagie representing Lagos State."

"I knew you would win," my coach said with a high five. I grinned, more cheers and congratulations coming my way as I climbed up the spectators sitting area and sat down to watch other races.

"You are from Bendel State!" It was a statement not a question. I looked up and recognised the Bendel State coach. "You are a Belo-Osagie, an Oloke? Which of the Belo-Osagies are you?"

"I am Alidu's daughter," I answered even though I wanted him to leave me alone. *Who was this man and why was he reminding me of my father?*

"Oh, I know your father; he is a policeman, right?"
I nodded.

"We want you to run for Bendel instead of Lagos. We will give you a scholarship," he said.

I took a sip of my Tree Top juice and politely answered, "I am on Lagos State Scholarship already, sir."

"Eee Ovbiedo vwe khin?" He looked surprised as he asked if I was not a Bini girl.

As I wondered how to get away from him and the conversation that was picking at wounds that had just started to scab, the gun went off for the 200 metres relay race. The roar and excitement from the crowd as they stood drowned his voice, giving me a chance to escape down the bleachers. I was only about twelve years old, but I already knew what I was going to do with the rest of my life, or so I thought. I would run hurdles and be like Modupe Oshikoya, one of Nigeria's best athletes in hurdles, relays, and sprints. When I was in Form 1, she had been in Form 3 or 4, and although most of us were too timid to approach our seniors—it could earn a junior girl a rebuff or even punishment—she was every girl's school mother desire. She was my inspiration when I started running hurdles. By the time I was in Form 3, she was already representing Nigeria in International Athletics, carting away gold medals and breaking world records. I was in awe of her talent and all I wanted was to be the next Modupe Oshikoya.

I seemed really close to the dream too. I was so good at hurdles that, one day, when the honourable Commissioner of Education, Chief Adeniran Ogunsanya, visited my school, Methodist Girls High School, Yaba, and announced a scholarship grant for some of the school's students; my name was among the grantees. It was a dream come true as it meant that my mum, who was raising us alone, did not have to worry about my tuition fees for two years. I could not wait to tell her about the scholarship and that I had qualified to go to Jos.

My father's family, The Belo-Osagies, and our cousins, the Giwa-Osagies, are influential families in Benin—we are known as the Olokes. My father, Alidu Belo-Osagie, was a policeman, so my earliest memories are of fun times in our home at the police barracks in Obalende. Our accommodation, Block 13 Room 17, was a room and a parlour. The barracks was communal; on our floor, we all shared a common kitchen and bathrooms. I remember it being so homely—

those were the days when attention was paid to the barracks and welfare of policemen. Our balcony, on the second floor, was a good spot from which my siblings and I would often watch what was happening in the barracks and outside. Right across from us was St. Gregory's School, where we attended church bazaars and watched children play soccer.

As a child, I would walk from the barracks to my school, St. Mathias Primary School, in Lafiaji. I looked forward to the breaks at noon, when the bell would ring and we would rush to the corridor to recite the Angelus. Even though my family was Muslim, my father was liberal and I found that I loved reciting the Hail Marys. Then would come lunch and I'd rush down to the most popular vendor in school to buy rice and the head of fish. The delicacy was the head, and if it had finished by the time it was my turn to buy food, I would be so sad. After school, I would walk back home, often with my friends who were also from the barracks and went to the same school or other schools in the area.

In the years before my dad transferred to Benin, we would sometimes visit other family members who lived in what my little eyes saw as mansions, in Ikoyi. Although Ikoyi and Obalende were so close, the difference in status was clear.

I was close to E'baba, as we called my dad. We shared a lot, down to our 'k-legs' and athleticism. He often served as the referee on the Police football team, and whenever I got to watch one of those matches, my chest would swell in pride as he ran across the field. Even now, I can still picture him in his black referee uniform,

left hand in the air, right hand holding a whistle to his lips as he prepared to caution a player.

"That's my daddy," I'd say to anyone close enough to hear. He really was a handsome man with curly dark hair.

Every day before he headed out to his duty post, we would take turns to shine his boots until we could see our reflection, as he instructed. He would always return home bearing gifts like pastry, almond fruits or local apples from wherever he had gone to work overnight. They were treats my siblings and I looked forward to.

Father was doting; he didn't take lightly to bullying. He would come to school with us to bully our bullies, so we became notorious as children of a father who took care of bullies. He was our first hero, and everyone around for miles knew it. I remember a time when he went on a peacekeeping mission and came back with two Alsatians. I was so excited that I jumped from the first floor balcony, breaking my fall on a ledge. Everyone stared in horror as I finally embraced Father with a limp. I could have broken a leg and it wouldn't have mattered. What mattered was that daddy was home. Now, I wonder how he had managed to return from a peacekeeping mission with dogs that were not even local to the region.

My mum (or Iye as we like to call her) was a seamstress, so we were always well turned out, whether it was at home or to birthday parties where so many children would eat rice and stew with chicken heads

12

and feet, from a *basia* – a huge tray – and wash it down with soft drinks; those were fun times for us in the barracks.

I don't recall why Mum left or why my parents got separated. My eldest sister, Gloria, and I have different accounts of what exactly happened. From the time Mum left, things changed and dad changed too. And then came our stepmother. Unlike the stepmothers I had read about in slim story books, Dad's new wife was kind and gentle. She addressed us as *ọkọ mi* (my husband), never calling us by our names even though we were kids and she was much older than we were.

I can't remember how old I was when it happened; time seems to have blurred my memory. Perhaps I was between six and eight years old. As usual, I had gone to school with my brother, Fred; my job was to see that he has settled well in his school before going to mine. We walked back home from school to see a truck parked outside our house. Somewhere in the vicinity were two bulging bags, which I later realised contained our stuff. It did not raise my concern until I saw Father come out of the house carrying furniture and loading it onto the truck.

"Are we going somewhere?" I asked.

"Good that you're back from school. *Ya vba iyu wa.* Go to your mum," he replied as he pressed money into my hand.

The response left me dissolving in tears. Fred, unsure what was happening but seeing his big sister crying, joined in. Father had been transferred, so he and his wife were relocating to Benin without us.

We had been just in time to see him drive out of our lives forever. As the truck raced off and raised a cloud in its wake, I tasted dust and then the tears freely flowed. I tried to wave but my right hand felt paralysed as I held tight to my baby brother who, earlier that week, had suffered another of his sickle-cell crises.

As what innocence was left in my childhood ended abruptly, my brother and I stood there wondering what was going on until a commune of women gathered around us. The comments started, ending with questions.

"Do you know where your mother is?"

"Yes, we visited her in Alagomeji, Yaba," I answered.

"Do you know the address?"

"If we get to Alagomeji, I know how to walk there from the bus stop."

The women took us to the bus stop closest to the barracks at Obalende, and put us on a bus, giving the bus conductor strict instructions about watching over us and making sure we got off at Alagomeji

"When you get to Alagomeji, tell him, Ó wà oo," one of the women said to me.

It was time to go live with Mum.

At Alagomeji, my brother and I got off the bus, and we walked down Hughes Avenue and onto Akinwunmi Street, counting the houses until we got to number 47, where Mum lived. Mum was shocked to see us; she wasn't expecting us. She tried to find an answer on our faces and finding none, she asked why we had come visiting on a school day and with what seemed like all our belongings. At that moment, I began to sob and then I wailed as what had happened dawned on Mum and me. Between sobs, I explained that father sent us away and travelled to Benin. Seeing his sister crying again, Fred began to sob too. Mum stayed calm, she didn't betray any emotions. I am not really sure where Gloria and Barbara were at this time. It is all a blur now. After a good meal and soft drinks we became calmer as mother assured us that father would return to get us. Years later I understood it was my father's way of getting even with Mum for leaving him. It just happened that we found ourselves in the crossfire. After Father left, all the responsibilities for caring for four of us children fell on my mother, and she worked herself to the bone to do so.

The train ride to Jos filled me with wonder. I was elated, as I had never travelled anywhere before. Being on a train was a big adventure for a young girl like me, and I could not wait to race against the other athletes and take the cup home for Lagos State. Back in school, my Physical Education classes had been all the training I got, so I looked forward to running at a national level because I had built up this experience in my head that there would be a proper camp and training for us as if we were professional athletes. However, it didn't quite happen that way. Years later, whenever Nigerian sports-people complained about the lack of care and attention during international games, I would remember how I had once imagined that we would be spoilt silly at the camp.

When the moment I so longed for came, I took my position on the tracks as usual, eager to run and jump hurdles, eager to feel everything else fall behind me. The gun went off; I took off. The first hurdle was down; the second hurdle was down; then, as I tried to scale the third hurdle, I suddenly felt a sharp pain in my side, so intense that I couldn't scale anymore hurdles. I had to stop. I was later told that it was just a muscle pain; something most athletes are familiar with. I was sad I lost out on that competition as I had had great hopes of returning to Lagos with a medal.

Back in Lagos, I still took part in a few races for my school, I even tried the javelin but gradually, my dream to be the next Modupe Oshikoya fizzled out. Perhaps it was also a good time for me to face my academics squarely because about that time, my grades had begun to drop. I was not surprised when I was told that I had to repeat a class. I dreaded telling my mum about being told to repeat. Surprisingly, she took it well. The life of a single mum was a hard knock life for her and for us, and that was why I felt pained when, because of a slight misdemeanour in class, one of my teachers had retorted, "I am not surprised. That is how children of single mothers behave." I was thrown off balance by such venom. Who was she to talk about my mum like that? When I got to the class in which I could choose my subjects, I ditched hers even though I was very good at the subject she taught.

The day after I had told my mum about repeating a class, I did the hopscotch all the way to school with mum's encouraging words ringing in my ears, *the fact that you are repeating a class does not make you a dullard.* I told myself, *yes, I had failed a class, but that didn't make me a failure.* That attitude changed everything and I regained my confidence and became more determined to work harder, to focus more on my classwork. My love for athletics still burned within me, so I attended school inter-house sports whenever I had the opportunity.

Years later, after my A levels, I got admitted into the University of Lagos to study English and Philosophy. The university was a whole new ball game. It came with its own challenges, and I found myself drinking a lot of coffee to stay awake to study. I was very determined to graduate at the top of my class.

CHAPTER 2

WOMEN. A FORCE

The house at 47 Akinwunmi Street, Yaba, holds many memories. It was where I spent the later part of my childhood. It was where I started learning to deal with the circumstance that led us to live with Mum. The house was a typical Nigerian face-me-I-face-you with a long, often poorly lit corridor down the middle, and rooms on either side, so that one tenant's door faced another's. The cramped buildings were famed for spats between tenants, hence the name. We had gone from our room and parlour apartment in the barracks to the one room mum rented when we first joined her. In the room, there was one bed for my mum and Fred, and a mattress on the floor for my sisters and me. After the tenant across from our room moved out, we upgraded as mum rented the room so we could share both. Like in the barracks, we shared the kitchen down the corridor with other neighbours. The bathroom was at the back of the building, and in the first few months, during power outages, I would be terrified to go there, especially because a neighbour had spread a rumour about seeing a ghost there once.

Mum stepped into her sole-parent role effortlessly. To ensure that we remained on the straight and narrow path, she never spared the whip. She was the typical Nigerian mother right down to the

19

ìgbájú and *ìgbátí*. Mum had a way of ensuring that we did not slack on any errand. She would spit on the floor and threaten that if the spit dried before we got back, our belly button would fall off. We were too young and naive to question the correlation between dry spittle and the belly button but it worked well for Mum. She would dust off her Singer sewing machines and churn out lovely dresses, uniforms and bed sheets, for commercial purchase. One thing my siblings and I were known for in the neighbourhood, was our sense of fashion. As a seamstress, Mum decked us up like dolls. We were the children of the owner of UWA fashion house. I remember this one 'baby doll' dress she made for me. It was the most beautiful shade of blue, but even its colour was secondary to the craft – oh, the number of tiers that decorated it! They rolled and rolled, each embellished tier adding volume to my twiggy frame. Another memory is the image of my siblings and I sporting white pairs of shorts over white tees; imaginary lawn tennis professionals! And ah, I remember a thigh-length mini skirt she made for me...oh, I got a few good stares when I finished the look off with the seventies style afro chic, wearing chunky platforms.

I remember how Mum would use a hot comb placed over an open fire to stretch our hair. Most times, our ears would get stretched as well. It was something we both loved and dreaded as our kinky natural hair gave way to straight hair.

Looking back now, there is no doubt that my siblings and I got our tenacity and grit from our mother. To keep up with our needs, Mum worked two jobs. One was as a connecting lady at Nigerian

External Telecoms, the other, as a staff of the Nigerian Tobacco Company. In between, she found time to handle her other business. She would sit at her sewing machine late at night, making the bed sheets, uniforms and dresses for her many clients. Her mummy-duties were endless; she was a machine just like her Singer.

"You will go and deliver these bed sheets to Kingsway tomorrow after school," she would say to me. Usually, thirty days after delivering to the stores, I would return to pick up cheques and more LPOs (local purchase orders).

I would usually frown and moan, "Why does it have to be me all the time? Why not Gloria? Why not Barbara?" But, even as a child, I knew that was what put food on our table. I knew most of the stores on Broad Street, Lagos, because often, I had made deliveries to Chellarams, Leventis, Bhojsons, and UTC. I really didn't like doing these errands, it made me feel like the Cinderella in the house. Mum made me do more chores than my siblings. I was the delivery girl, the laundry girl, and the cook. I cooked so much that I swore that when I got married, I would not cook, and God answered that prayer when I met my husband who never demands that I cook his meals. So, you could say I am one of those women who don't 'do kitchen.'

Watching my mum, I got to understand the value of hard work, I also got to understand that many women were not afforded the sensitivity of emotions and chill days because they were holding up whole families by their shoulders, raised, not in pride but from the burden of keeping destinies from crashing to the ground.

Christmas had always been a big deal back in the barracks. My dad was totally sold on the holiday and its merriment. He was one to acquire fireworks days before Christmas, and we all imbibed the culture of sending Christmas cards. On Christmas Eve, Dad would bring out his bag of fireworks, excited like a young boy who was happy at the prospects of a new toy. We would light up the biscos – a popular childish lingo for 'firecrackers' – and shoot the fireworks, and then, we would all run around both excited and afraid of the sparkling fire.

I wondered if my friends back at the barracks missed me, and if they had seen any Èyọ̀ processions since we left. The Èyọ̀ masquerade, a major cultural celebration of Lagos, was one of the rare but wonderful sights that had us in awe as children. They wore wide-brimmed hats that covered their heads and veils over their faces that flowed into the rest of their gleaming white outfits. We saw no skin, not even their hands that held the staff as they danced and leaped along their way. Although we were scared of them because adults told us they were deities, we would stand on our balcony and watch them file past. The brave children among us would go downstairs and try to watch from the front of the barracks, until one of the adults noticed and chased them back indoors. For days after, we would sing the songs as they did,

'Èyọ̀ o, eh, Èyọ̀ o
Èyọ̀ Baba tàwa tó fi gólù seré
Àwa ò ní sanwó oníbodè

Ó di 'lé
Ẹníjalè, ẹníja lè lóbọmọjẹ́.
Kí la fi gbé,
Owó, owó lafi gbé,
Kí lo fi rà,
Aṣo, aṣo lo fi rà, aho kí lorà,
Èye, èye òyinbó...'

We would try to dance and leap like them and even mimic their incantations.

As children, Mum spoilt us with comics and story books. My favourite author was Charles Hamilton – creator of one of my favourite book characters, Bessy Bunter. We loved the books so much that we adopted names from them. We changed the names we had been given at birth to the names we each go by up till now. My parents were so liberal they took to calling us by the new names we had chosen.

The high point of our Christmas after our father left was the joy of receiving Christmas cards from him every year. Each Christmas period, we would stand outside looking for the postman, and squeal as he went through his mailbag to hand us the cards from our father. We would immediately recognise the handwriting. As the years rolled by, the cards gradually stopped coming.

"Maybe it got lost," Mum said once, after I asked her, "Why did the cards stop coming?"

By this time, I had learnt to live in the moment, to find joy all around me. I had managed to put the past behind and allow the healing process to begin, or so I thought. I was making new friends, and we had moved into a proper apartment – a 3-bedroom flat on Adébíyí Street, Yaba, around where Hubert Ògúndé the famous Nigerian actor, playwright, theatre manager and musician lived, right behind us. Noble Street was where the Ògúndé Travelling Theatre was based. It was the first contemporary theatre in Nigeria, which was a forerunner to the modern Nigerian film industry now called Nollywood. Many times, when rehearsals were going on, we would strain our ears to enjoy the cultural percussions. Especially as they sang:

'Wọn pa Lumumba
Wọn pa Lumumba...'

This song was a tribute to Patrice Lumumba, Congo's first prime minister who was assassinated on January 17, 1961.

Another favourite of mine from Ògúndé was *Yorùbá Ronú*, a musical drama which satirized the political leaders of the then Western Region with songs, dance, and sketches. It was written and performed after Chief Ọbáfẹ́mi Awólọ́wọ̀ was arrested and jailed for treason and his deputy, Chief Akíntọ́lá replaced him as the Premier. The play was eventually banned around Yorùbá land by the Akíntọ́lá Government for its explicit politically provocative content. The ban was overturned when Chief Ọbáfẹ́mi Awólọ́wọ̀ was released from prison in August 1966.

Then, there was the tragic death of Ogunde's wife, Adesewa, which was a sad day indeed. We knew even as children because the songs turned mournful.

My life settled into a new rhythm, brightening once again. I was eleven years old, and I was starting Form One at Methodist Girls' High School, Yaba. I was happy to make new friends, embrace a new beginning. I was especially happy we had left our face-me-I-face-you at Akinwunmi. The only reservation I had was that at Adebiyi, there were no open gutters where I could go crab hunting as I used to at Akinwunmi. Red crabs could be found in the gutter that ran in front of the house when it rained. So, at 5am, we children would go crab fishing, catching them then tying them up so that their pincers could not pinch us. In the morning, we would arrange them in a bowl in front of the house so passers-by could buy. The thrill of catching crabs and trying to avoid getting pinched was so great that we barely paid attention to how much we made from it.

I often think about how true it is that life only makes sense when you look at it in retrospect. There are many things I had no words for when I was growing up, and so had no real understanding of at the time. Like how my mum had trouble sleeping.

"Betty!"
"Ma."
"Doh, n'iye m owe," she'd say. 'Come and stretch my toes.'

I'd respond and I'd quietly stomp my feet as I walked over to her bed to obey the instructions she had given in Bini. I would take one foot in hand, and then gently massage each toe in turn until she fell asleep. My siblings and I dreaded this task and we often feigned sleep once she headed for bed, otherwise, one could be on her bed, foot in hand for up to two hours. And then, the minute you try to get up, hoping her silence was because she had fallen asleep, she'd say,

"De ke nu rie. Where are you going?"
We would doze off on her bed with her.

So involved had we been in her sleeplessness that long after that, I often recalled the image of her sleepless while we massaged her foot. I didn't know it was called insomnia, or that it would trouble me too in future. A few years ago, when I first started to reflect a lot about my childhood and young adulthood, I thought about how a lot of the happenings in my early life created or pointed to patterns. Yet, like a jigsaw puzzle made up of millions of tiny pieces, it was impossible to know the full picture until the pieces were placed side by side deliberately and fitted together.

When I first started to have trouble sleeping in my late twenties, I still did not make the connection that it was like what my mum had dealt with while I was young. It started shortly after I got married at twenty-seven. After a few sleepless nights, I took to buying Valium over the counter at the pharmacy. I took Valium for many years, constantly wishing I was one of those people who fell asleep as soon as their heads touched their pillows or even fell asleep in meetings and public gatherings till they snored and were nudged awake. I didn't know then that I should have been grateful for those few hours of sleep I got each night.

⟍

My fiftieth birthday was a wonderful reminder of how far I had come in life and how God had blessed me beyond my imagination. It was one of the most memorable events of my life.

Fifty was such a milestone that I wanted to mark it in the best way possible. I was hardly involved in planning the celebration; we had a planner, FVO, who worked with my husband. She planned every detail from the venue to the guests' seating arrangements, and the menu. A few days before the party, I had a fitting at my designer's and as she pinned the sides of the outfit a little, she remarked, "Betty, I think you have lost a lot of weight. The last time I measured you, you were not this slim."

"I have noticed as well. I think it's because I am not getting enough sleep." But even at that, I wasn't that worried because I was getting a lot of compliments about looking fab at fifty. And, I did look gorgeous on that day, in my red and gold number. The look was exactly what I wanted, body glistening from a dose of body scrubs and exfoliation at the spa, make up was perfect. My gold ruched aṣo-òkè tube top over a red skirt with fringes that celebrated my every move was a statement piece. I literally sparkled. The dress code was red and gold and my guests did not disappoint. More than being my birthday, it looked like a celebration of fashion, one of my favourite things.

By the time the party was in full swing, the venue was bustling with family and friends. The night had so many highlights.

Then a saxophone sounded, and I looked around, wondering what was going on. I spotted the Masked One. I squealed. It was Lágbájá. So, that was the big surprise my husband and the event planner had up their sleeve!

Everyone gave himself or herself permission to be silly and have fun, so we danced in circles, drank, ate and joked heartily as the party went on till the wee hours of the morning.

If my birthday is any indication, my 50s are going to be the adventure of my life, I thought. I did not know just how correct that statement would be, or that adventures aren't always a fun ride.

↓

I savoured every moment of my life in those days. I had a wonderful and supportive husband, my children were in university and already carving good paths for themselves through life, and I ran a magazine that was thriving against all odds four years after I started it. Nothing could stop my roll, I believed.

In 2009, the year I turned fifty-two, my period stopped. Of course that was not a surprise. From my Biology classes, I had been taught that at menopause, every woman would stop seeing her monthly period. Over the years, during some periods, I had even looked forward to menopause. I had often joked with friends that I couldn't wait to stop bleeding every month, carrying pads about, dealing with the cramps and other random aches that came with each period.

"We women really try," I'd say. "Because as soon as we finish dealing with bleeding and cramps each month, we have to count down to ovulation days and the symptoms that can come with that too. Then the premenstrual symptoms window, which is always like a roller-coaster both emotionally and physically."

When it came, I realised nothing prepared me for it. It wasn't a gradual reduction or intermittent periods, as I'd believed it would be; it just stopped completely. I should have been relieved, but there was no time for that as many things began to happen. Surprisingly, I did not experience hot flashes, which is a major symptom of menopause. In a way, I was relieved because I had become accustomed to seeing women sweating even in highly air-conditioned rooms. It was a common sight to see women who were going through menopause hold towels to dab their faces as bouts of hot flashes overwhelmed them. What I got instead was chronic insomnia. My already poor sleep pattern got worse and I would have mood swings. One minute, I would be up and about, happy, and the next, I'd feel so low in spirit. Of course, many women who experience PMS know this is familiar monthly. Since it wasn't very intense at first, I didn't worry, and because nobody really talked about menopause, I didn't know what was going on with my body.

When sleep became more elusive than before, worry started to nibble at the corners of my mind. I would go for days with only a few hours of sleep, and the mood swings would intensify.

"I don't know what is going on," I confessed to a close friend one day. "My sleep pattern has become worse. I am cranky and moody."

"Oh, I hear Hormone Replacement Therapy could help with hormonal balance. Would you like to try it out?" she said.

"How would you know?" I teased, "You are not even there yet." We both laughed.

Then, she said more seriously, "One of my aunts went through menopause, and she had to be placed on HRT so she wouldn't lose her mind. You know what, Betty? When I get to menopause, and it becomes as problematic as my aunt's, I am not going to hesitate to go on HRT." At that point, I told her why I was afraid of hormone replacement therapy. Alarm bells went off in my head. Because of my work in breast cancer advocacy over the years, I knew there was a link between HRT and breast cancer. I got to know more about this after I started the Genevieve Pink Ball foundation. The Pink Ball was Genevieve's cancer awareness advocacy which we had founded soon after the magazine took off. It was a purpose that found us. We were already telling the stories of women's successes and struggles, but when I realised the level of ignorance regarding breast cancer in Nigeria, and that we could use our platform to begin the narrative on such a treacherous health issue that affects women, we decided to launch the Pink Ball Foundation.

I'll just have to weather this, I told myself.

The mood swings persisted and got worse, but in spite of everything, I managed to keep *Genevieve* going even though it was taking a toll on my health. I would sit at editorial meetings, edit all hundred pages of the magazine, supervise photo shoots, design layouts, distribution, and chase advertisements and sales... the life of an entrepreneur.

As the days passed, I began to have more moments when it felt like someone had locked me in a dark room without light and I was stumbling about trying to find my way. I would feel heavy and sad, but then I might have a really good day that brushed off the feeling of heaviness. I didn't pay any more attention to it until my body began to change. I panicked when my weight plummeted further. I could not understand what was happening. I lost my appetite and often subsisted on little bites. One morning, I tried on a dress that used to fit me snugly but, in the mirror, it looked like someone had draped a huge sack around my body. I had lost so much weight in a few months that many of my previously fitted outfits began to sag. Alarmed, I turned to another friend who referred me to her own doctor. The next day, I decided to see my friend's doctor who she said had helped her through her own struggles when she went into menopause at forty-six.

Sitting in front of the doctor, I felt calm, especially as he had assured me that in no time at all, I would be as good as new. I was excited about the prospect of having my life back, and I couldn't wait.

"Let me share a secret with you," said the doctor. "I have the perfect remedy for you. This injection will make you feel younger, look younger, and regulate your mood. Most of the women that you see around, the celebrities and socialites who are going through what you are going through, are on this injection," he informed me with a smug smile.

My ears perked up. Menopause was going to be a breeze like I'd always hoped it would be, after all. I could almost taste the relief of being able to be and look myself again.

"So, what is it?" I asked curiously. He tried to explain in medical gibberish; it was all jargon to me.

"In short, we call it the 'joy' injection," he said.

If he could have heard what was going on inside of me, it would have sounded like a little girl jumping and squealing, "Yay, give me!"

I took the injection with a little bit of apprehension despite my excitement. Almost immediately, I began to feel that sense of joy he had spoken about. I went back home happier. That week, I got so much done on the Genevieve edition we were working on. It was as if someone had indeed turned on a joy switch and I was excited about life again. I was so upbeat that my best friend, Barbara, noticed during our next phone chat.

"Oh, I took this injection," I said with excitement, quickly telling her about my visit to the doctor and how much better it had made me feel. She was one of the few who knew about my menopause experience so I was happy to share the good news with her.

"Really," she replied. "Oh and you didn't tell me about it. What is the name of the injection?"

"The doctor said it's the joy injection," I replied.

"Oh! That explains your upbeat mood. I better go and see the doctor myself."

After Barbara's visit to the doctor, she called me. I had looked forward to hearing that it had made her feel better too, so I was surprised when she said,

"I didn't take the injection."
"But why?" I asked.
"It's a steroid," she all but exclaimed.

I don't remember what my response to her was but I remember feeling very panicky. I had been so eager to feel relief from pain that I had not asked the doctor questions to know what exactly made up "the joy injection". Barbara, who had a degree in Chemistry, was the one who had been more cautious. The doctor had told me I would have to take the injection periodically but, of course, I never went back to him. The experience left me withdrawn for days as I imagined that I could have been injected with anything—something even worse than steroids and their many side effects—and I wouldn't have known because I hadn't asked even though I had paid a lot of money for it. It was a good thing that experience happened early on as it taught me to be more analytical, to ask questions and research any drugs or treatment options I was offered.

The next doctor I saw about my situation also suggested Hormone Replacement Therapy.

"It will help with the chemical imbalance as well as the side effects of menopause," he explained.

"No," I said.

"Why?" he pressed.

After I told him about my fears, he explained that the HRT treatment he had suggested was nature-based. However, the pamphlets he gave me about the treatment also warned about breast cancer, listing it as a potential side effect.

"Let me get back to you about it," I said to him, not willing to jump into anything so soon after my steroids experience.

Before I left the clinic, he gave me some hormone creams to rub on my ankles and chest so that my body would absorb them and regain some of the hormones that I had lost due to menopause.

It didn't. I still continued to toss at night and lose weight. Even the thought of how long the menopause experience might last started to cause my chest to tighten in anxiety daily. Sleeplessness had brought in what I would later learn was its sibling, anxiety. While mulling over if I should give in and take HRT, at random moments sitting at work or at home, I'd suddenly ask myself: "Which one would you rather have? Cancer or this mid-life crisis brought on by menopause?" I decided to try out the HRT.

Eighteen months into the HRT prescriptions, I found a lump in one of my breasts. Thankfully, after tests were carried out the lump turned out to be benign...but so much else happened before that.

34

CHAPTER 3

WE'RE IN THIS TOGETHER

One day, sometime in 2010, I visited my friend Toks Keks with whom I have been friends since my teenage years. Our friendship has carried over to our children, and together, we have kept the bond going.

She ushered me into her dining room, and as we ate, she noticed my mood and tried to draw me into a conversation. She looked up and asked, "Sho gbúròó Sonia? When was the last time you heard from Sonia?"

I kept quiet as my thoughts flitted back and forth through my many hospital visits in the past year, and my eyes smarted as tears began to well up in them, Poor Sonia didn't know the enormity of what I was going through, I wanted to save her that trauma. I blinked rapidly and raised my right hand, trying to fan air into my eyes so that they wouldn't get red. I hoped she wouldn't notice the tears, but we were too close for her not to notice that something was utterly wrong. She was alarmed and gently whispered, "Let's go into the garden," because she did not want her husband to see me cry.

"What's the matter?" She kept asking. "Whatever it is, you can tell me."

"I'm fine," I sniffed, trying to control the emotions that had suddenly overwhelmed me. As she fussed over me, I realised it was time to let her know what I was battling with. She wasn't the kind of friend I could lock out of that moment in my life, so I opened up to her. She couldn't believe what I had been going through silently.

"Good morning, Betty," Soni's happy voice came from his side of the bed.

I wasn't asleep when he came in the night before, but because I didn't want him to see me the way I was, I had pulled the covers over my head and lain still, hoping I'd fall asleep. I had somehow hoped he would go out early and not try to talk to me. I should have known better, after twenty-seven years of daily morning conversations. *If I talk to him, he will take his shower and go out,* I thought, so I eased the covers down a little, holding them to my chin.

"Morning," I mumbled.

Instead of going to the bathroom, he looked down at me then sat on my side of the bed.

"What's wrong?" he asked, concerned. "You didn't sleep again?

I shook my head and a tear dropped from my eyes. He wiped the tears from my face. He sat closer, touching my hair.

"Should we go and see a doctor?" Beyond his voice, I could see the worry on his face. He stood up to make a call.

"I won't come in today," I soon heard him saying to someone on the phone, and I realised he was calling his office to cancel his appointments. Soni has always been like that. Every time I had malaria or typhoid in the past, he was the one to take me to the hospital. He never compromised on the care and health of his family.

He put down the phone and said to me, "Betty, what is the matter?"

How was I going to explain that I felt out of control of my own body and my life was falling apart as I could not seem to do anything but free float through each day. I felt like a piece of scrap caught adrift, being blown wherever the wind pleased. It didn't make sense to me no matter how much I tried to figure it out, so how was I going to explain it to someone else?

But, the thing with Soni is that he is always patient. No matter how long it took for me to explain how I was feeling, he would be patient.

"Whatever it is, we are in this together you know," It wasn't the first time he had told me that.

When Soni walks into a room, it's always as though he's brought some extra light in with him. One just gravitates towards his brightness. Over the years, his sunny disposition had helped me to get through a lot of moments that would have otherwise been dreary. He always had the perfect joke for me or the wisdom I needed to be calm.

Between his great sense of humour and his love for me—and then our kids when they came—I had never once felt like my world was falling apart, until now, when his attempts to make me share what I was going through didn't work. Sadly, he could no longer tease me into laughter.

We didn't have one of those meet-cute stories. In fact, when I first noticed him during my years studying English in Unilag, *I thought, who does he think he is?* At the time, I was in my early twenties and he was already a media personality, so on the few occasions I saw him at Matthew's Buttery on campus, there were girls vying to talk with him or be seen with him.

"A Bini man," I would laugh with my friends. "God forbid."

I was sure that even if the world somehow ran out of single men, I would never marry a Bini man. I often said they were unromantic, so in those years – and even after we first met properly – I was convinced I would have nothing to do with Soni.

Back then, I was working as a rookie public relations officer. My company, which was a recording company, had an album launch event coming up, and the CEO said to me, "You're the Public Relations Officer; it's your job to get the media there."

Okay. I thought. *I'm going to get sacked after I mess this up because I don't know anyone in media and I don't know anything about media.*

I explained my dilemma to the CEO's Romanian PA who was also my friend.

"There is this celebrity guy," she said. "He's like a Nigerian Robert Redford, just that he is a radio presenter not an actor. He's coming in today, and he may be able to help."

That afternoon, when I saw the person she had described using the famous American actor, all I thought was, *Okay he's cool, but I used to see him in Unilag; very arrogant Bini guy.* By that time, he had his Sunday Show on NTA. I had never spoken to him before that day but, just from seeing him occasionally, I had been sure he was full of himself.

I stood close to her desk, taking notes as she asked him for pointers. He was kind and he patiently gave tips on what to do, whom to contact, and how to ensure the event was properly publicised. I didn't meet him formally that day.

At the album launch, I was busy but noticed he was there with two of his friends. They were obviously having a good time as they laughed really loud.

The event went superbly, until it was time for me to give the vote of thanks. I took the microphone and said a few words until I became overwhelmed with fear...the fear of public speaking. My hands began to shake and my heartbeat increased. I was so embarrassed that I dropped the microphone and ran upstairs right in the middle of making the speech. The fear of public speaking trailed my life for nearly four decades, but today, there is nothing I love more than speaking in public.

Later, when I calmed down and was less overwhelmed with shame, I tried to mingle with the crowd. Soni came up to me, led me outside, and because it was drizzling, we went into his car and sat down to talk.

First, he assured me that I hadn't done too badly, and I shouldn't worry about my fear of speaking, because I would get better in time. Then, he revealed that when he came in, he had asked one of his friends: "Who is she?"

"Betty Belo-Osagie," his friend had replied.

"Na this girl I go marry o. Make I go find out first who she really be," he told them.

And so, the friendship started.

He came to my office a few days later and said, "I'd like to take you out. I'd like to see you another time if you're available."

"That would be nice," I said.

As I started getting to know him, I realised just how far off the mark I had been about my assessment of him from my Unilag days. His grit showed in everything, and I was not surprised when he told me he had come to Lagos as a seventeen-year-old, determined to make his own way. He had worked at the Prisons as a social worker, before he established himself as a broadcaster on Radio Nigeria and later began to host Soni Irabor live.

Our first date was at Bar Beach, and then we went to Ikoyi Park with my brother, Ṣèyí, in tow. The words he had spoken to his friends would prove true as we struck a relationship and got married exactly a year later in July 1983.

If I doubted that I had caught feelings for Soni while we dated, the weeks leading to our marriage convinced me I had made the right choice. We had set the date and made arrangements when his family said if my father would not be at the wedding, it would not be right for his family to attend, especially as my father was still alive. They tried to put pressure on Soni and I to invite him, but I refused to do so. I was still smarting from how he had acted when my sister, Gloria, got married. She had sent him an invitation, which he had turned down. When my uncle volunteered to give her away in his place, he confronted my uncle and asked, "Who gave you a daughter?" Father later said to the man, "Look at you giving out a daughter who isn't yours when their father is still alive."

I did not want to put myself through the pain of a refusal and put whoever stood in his place through the rudeness of being taunted, so I told Soni I was not going to invite him. Early on in our relationship, I had opened up to Soni about the strain in our relationship with our father.

His father, on the other hand, did not have this back story, so he convinced me to go with him to see my father. Soni, his dad, and I, went to visit my dad at his home. He lived on Akpakpava Street in Benin. Sitting there face to face with my dad, for the first time since he left, I had mixed emotions. If he was happy to see me, he didn't show it, but he was civil enough to receive us. Sadly, our mission towards reconciliation did not yield the desired fruit. I felt a further sense of loss. Right there, I made up my mind, he wasn't welcome to my wedding. At the end of that visit, I realised some things were better left the way they were.

"We'll do the registry, and we can do the church wedding later," Soni said to me when we left.

I think, in a way, the bond of our marriage was further strengthened as we realised that we were doing it alone without the support of his family – who had backed out in other to fulfil tradition. Soni was never one to cower before any one, as long as he was convinced he was doing the right thing. And that, for me, was a glimpse into how our marriage was going be. I knew I was marrying someone who had my back, and in a way, the template was set for how we lived our lives as a couple. Soni was so protective, and he ensured there was no backlash on the decision that I had taken.

Soni and I decided to go see a doctor who asked all the questions concerning the history of my insomnia and moodiness, occasionally pausing to look at Soni, as if he could find an answer from his expression.

"Can you describe how you're feeling, madam," he said. I looked through him as if he was transparent, and I said nothing. The thing was, I didn't really know how I was feeling. I just wanted to be in the room alone, with the covers over my head, but Soni cajoled me into responding to the doctor.

"It started with me being tired all the time, and being unable to sleep. I don't know why but even when I'm hungry, I can't eat. I don't feel good, I don't look good, I am losing too much weight, and I don't know why, but I can't wave off this overwhelming feeling of sadness." I rushed out my words, afraid that if I thought too hard about them, it would be a jumble in my head again.

"How long have you battled with insomnia?" He asked.

"Most of my life," I replied. "I can't remember anytime I fell asleep in my adult life without a struggle and a little help from a pill."

He glanced toward Soni as if for a confirmation. Soni smiled wryly and nodded while I continued, "It just got worse when menopause set in."

"Okay, Madam. I am going to put you on these pills. I would also advise you to observe sleep hygiene: No TV in the room, take a warm bath, go to bed at the same time every night, switch off all devices, don't take work home, and do your breathing exercises to help your muscles relax."

The doctor wrote out a prescription, handed it to me and attempted a smile. Soni gave him a fifty thousand naira cheque, and we left.

I was back to the same doctor a month later because I still had more low days than high.

I sat across from him expecting some reprieve from this visit, but what I got instead...was a reprimand.

"You have to power up, madam." An alarm went off in my brain.

"Power up!" I looked up at him, and he stared back. "Power up!" I repeated, eyes blazing, nostrils flaring, enraged, looking for an outlet. I got up and reached for the door, but he stood in my way. He seemed to have suddenly realised how inappropriate his utterance was and he apologised. Later, he wrote a prescription. Which I took and muttered, "Thank you," and left.

In the course of my depression, one of my biggest challenges was having to explain to people that I was not on a weight-loss program. A newspaper even insinuated that I was anorexic. I remember reading that news item one Sunday morning and feeling so angry. It wasn't even a soft-sell magazine. My phone rang non-stop after that publication. Friends who had also wondered why I was losing weight suddenly seemed convinced that I was starving myself to look young. That incident further drove me into isolation.

I just wanted the world to stop so I could get off and catch my breath instead of running perpetually. It seemed there was no finish line and there was nothing to catch. At this stage, I had perfected the act of hiding away from my friends because I didn't want anybody to see how gaunt I looked, and those damn pigments on my face!

A couple of times when I braced myself to go out, especially on the red carpet, I would take a hand fan to cover my face. In no time at all, photo journalists began to resent and complain that I never allowed them to take a picture of me. If only they knew the battles I was fighting... the battle of low self-esteem and lack of confidence; a battle with self, a battle to stay alive.

By this time, I was tired of the various visits to, often times, clueless doctors. I was tired of misdiagnoses.

It's malaria, Madam... It's stress, Madam. You are just under a lot of pressure.

It seemed like the more doctors I saw, the worse my condition became. The total lack of empathy, as well as ignorance about mental health, floored me.

CHAPTER 4
MY LABOUR OF LOVE

I had taken to getting up every morning and forcing myself to go to the office, since all I did at home was feel sorry for myself. For the first two days back at work, I powered through tasks, taking on more and more to remind myself that I could get things done. On the third day, I had been sitting at my desk, head in hand for over thirty minutes before I finally opened my laptop. In the moment between when I opened it and gave it time to reboot, I saw my reflection on the screen. Anguish enveloped me, forcing me to shut the computer off immediately.

I had a Morning Dew column to turn in, but I didn't know what to write. I had spent some time on the phone talking to one of my sisters—anything to push away the tasks I needed to face. My siblings all knew I had been having trouble sleeping. In fact, it had become one of the recurring topics in our conversations and they constantly sent tips or remedies they thought might help.

I wanted to talk about what I was going through but I didn't even seem to have words for it. I thought about writing, but I seemed to have lost that gift. At this time, my biggest fear was that I might be seen as weak.

I wanted to write that for almost two years, I had gone through each day and night with anxiety and fear. I wanted to write that there were days when I wanted to step away from the magazine or shut it down, but I was scared. I was scared that if I stepped away, everything I had spent years building would come crumbling down. I was scared that if I shut it down I would have fallen into the statistic of people who had failed magazines. I had spent years telling people not to quit on their dreams, not to be afraid.

If you fail, I thought, you'll let many people down.

Genevieve had always been a validation of my courage, my determination. It had been the only thing that gave me succour, just knowing I built something from scratch. It has been inspirational across many generations. I had come too far to give it all up now. I had to keep going. I had to keep striving although someone told me a long time ago that the word 'to strive' is a negative energy that drains.

At the time, I didn't know that after almost eight years, my business should have been able to run smoothly without me. Even though I had groomed a team to handle Genevieve without me, I was still afraid to let go.

There are days so epochal in your life that you remember even the tiniest details about them. The day, in 2003, I conceived the idea that became Genevieve, is one of such. I remember that morning very clearly. Soni was away, and I was home alone that Saturday. I sat on the bedroom floor, foreign lifestyle magazines around me. I had always loved magazines, especially those focused on women—there is a richness of the female experience across age, race, and class that a great magazine offers. Yet, that day, I had surrounded myself with many because I had suddenly realised none of them spoke to the Nigerian experience, and every Nigerian woman knows there's a uniquely Nigerian female experience. I yearned to read profiles of strong Nigerian women and role models.

As someone once said, "if it doesn't exist, create it." I decided to create it. I needed confirmation that it needed to be done. I whispered to myself, "I can do this." That whisper was like speaking life into the unseen; it made me jump in excitement. I knew my next step, and I knew the vehicle that'd take me there. It was right with me in the house with me, a ubiquitous book I had had for 17 years but never read—we all have those books. In 1986, the United States Information Service (USIS) had sponsored Soni to go to 17 of its states. My son and I started the journey with him, but we remained in New York while he travelled to the other states. On his return to New York from one of those trips, he came back with a book—he always came bearing gifts. It was called 'The Magazine: Everything You Need to Know to Make It in the Magazine Business' by Professor Leonard Mogen.

"You like magazines, so I thought you might like a book about them," he said.

I only flipped through it; nothing in it piqued my interest. A book about making magazines was nowhere near as interesting as a magazine, I concluded. Back in Nigeria, I shelved it. Interestingly, everyone who saw it on my shelf and had a dream of publishing their magazine borrowed it. Sometimes, the borrower would not return it. It would be gone for years, and then, it would be returned to me. So it was on that Saturday in 2003, when I got the spark of an idea to create a lifestyle magazine for Nigerian women, the memory of the book followed my whisper and I got up to find it. I already knew what I should call my magazine, *Genevieve* – after my daughter, Sonia, whose birthday falls on the feast of St. Genevieve.

"Why do you want to publish a magazine at all?" People asked each time I shared my burning desire with them. "Publishing is not a job for women," they would say, and then, they'd remind me that I was forty-six.

I could understand where their thoughts came from. At the time I wanted to start *Genevieve,* I had a great job doing corporate promotions for multinationals. I had no real experience in publishing. I was just someone who had studied English and worked as a journalist for some years.

As a journalist in National Concord, as part of my assignment, I attended many magazine launches, but noticed sadly that most never made it to the 6th edition. They often succumbed to the third edition jinx. I would find out why when I started my magazine. It was due to inadequate funding opportunities, poor distributing network, reader and advertiser apathy, lack of infrastructure, and a preference for soft sell magazines.

At that time, many people said to me, "Why don't you publish a soft sell? Nigerians don't read." *Genevieve* would prove them wrong as reader apathy reduced. There was a jostling for *Genevieve*, and the advertisers began to trust us even though they was no real industry for luxury brands in Nigeria, as you would see in developed countries. So, we were dealing with a huge challenge in the form of lack of a structured industry that could support us. Distribution, as vital as it is to magazine publishing, was greatly affected by this disadvantage. Still, we made do. In the absence of fancy checkout counters, we put *Genevieve* on the streets with newspaper vendors. That was not without its own issues because some would sell the magazine and run off with the proceeds. There were agents that didn't reimburse us, and by the sixth edition, one of them had duped me of three million two hundred thousand naira. He had taken magazines for sale and had gone quiet for weeks.

"Has he remitted anything from sales?" I asked the office accountant one day. That was when we realised we hadn't received a dime from him in a while. By the time we tried to find him, we learnt he was on the run.

I was heartbroken.

Writing remained the sum of my experience in media publishing, until I read Leonard Mogen's book from cover to cover a few times. Once the idea for *Genevieve* took root, the book became my tutor, and Mogen himself vigorously coached me. Everything I learnt about publishing came from The Magazine. The book had been very clear about what was needed to successfully publish the type of magazine I wanted *Genevieve* to be—it listed a certain sum as starting capital. What I had was like 1% of what was advised. The book had been very specific in advising against starting with less. The book had also cautioned that publishing and restaurants had the highest rate of fatalities among all industries. I had all that at the back of my mind but I was not going to allow it to discourage me.

Everything was in my head. I had moments of uncertainty and anxiety. *Will I succeed or fail?*

I had titled all 100 standard pages of the magazine, and come up with a vision "to publish a magazine that was as aspirational as it was inspirational".

In all this, I can never downplay the role my team has had in helping to build and sustain the vision. The success of *Genevieve* was never dependent on one person. It has always been dependent on a formidable team which I later christened the G-team. *Genevieve* has always been about 'US' and not 'I'; 'WE' not 'ME'.

It has always been a labour of love.

A typical day in *Genevieve* is crazy; full of unpredictability. Anything can show up and throw a spanner in the works. It could be the exchange rate, a labour strike, photo shoots, unhappy advertisers, magazine theft, airport delays, or an editor or any other key staff resigning without any notice, I could go on and on.

Some days were however better than the rest. There were those exciting days when the feedback would make everything worth it. Other days, we agonised over shoddy jobs. Eventually we learnt to take the good with the bad.

I had to deal with constant anxiety and trepidation, sometimes in order to ease my anxiety and induce sleep, I would pop a Valium 5.

In the first two years, we were knocking off around 11pm or even 1am. Sometimes, my husband would bring the kids to the office to say goodnight. Sonia especially liked *Genevieve*. She was around thirteen at the time, and one day she asked if she could write for the magazine.

"Of course," I said, proud that she was keen to have her own column in the magazine. Little did I know that fourteen years after, she would step in as assistant editor, and now, editor. Before she did, my son, Omoruyi, had also held it down at *Genevieve*, as the General Manager. It was very emotional for me the day the baton exchanged hands and Sonia took over the mantle of editorship, giving the magazine the younger flavour it yearned for.

Sonia's early interest in publishing felt like a victory to me in the midst of the other daily battles I faced in the start-up journey. One of the toughest battles was getting advertising because advertisers had learnt that magazines didn't last, they were hesitant to put their investments in it.

Some covers came out awful, and there was an edition we turned into bonfire because it was so bad I didn't think we ought to circulate it. That day, I understood why the third edition jinx existed. Not only was magazine publishing capital intensive, in the beginning it was barely supported by sales or advertising.

Many times, I wanted to quit but I was so grateful I had read 'The Magazine.' I realised I was subconsciously prepared, I knew the whys. When the unexpected happened, I had moments of doubt, but when I remembered that it was expected, I held on to my boast in my first few Morning Dew editorial pages about finding my passion and not giving up no matter the challenges. I had assured myself that whenever you wake up is your morning. I had encouraged everyone to close their eyes, jump, and do it afraid. How could I then betray everyone by quitting?

It didn't get easier but I got stronger with every edition, even as each came with its peculiar stress.

It had been eight years since I went through the rollercoaster of starting *Genevieve*. We had been through so much and were still standing. That meant something, right? It had to mean something. I was supposed to be happy, proud, so why wasn't I? Why did each day come shrouded in darkness already? As if the sun could somehow reach the entire earth except the parts my body occupied. It was

2011, and I tried to recall the victories of the early days as despair stretched its jaw wider and wider to consume more of me each day.

"If you made it through those problems, you can make it through this constant tiredness and sleeplessness," I tried to tell myself. "If you didn't quit back then, you can't quit now and let down even more people than you would have at the time."

So, I continued to go to the *Genevieve* office every day. I would walk through the doors and drag my body and mind to the office, trying to coax myself into doing something. This was how it felt to me. However, this was not how it looked to others. I would be dressed in my usual stylish manner, wearing heels and, sometimes, shades to hide the dark circles under my eyes. I had to keep up appearances and I succeeded at this.

One Friday, I don't know how long I sat staring at the pink walls of my Ikoyi office. I barely registered the faint chatter coming from the creative office. I had just finished talking to an angry advertiser and I knew the team was fielding calls from others, including subscribers who were displeased by the late delivery that month. The week before, I had found out that a batch of Genevieve magazines was still at the cargo shed seven days after they arrived from Dubai.

"My advert is dated," a client complained. "The event is two days away," the advertiser had repeated to me over the phone, his voice rising louder each time.

I could not say anything. I had personally assured him that it would be out a week before his corporate event, so when it arrived the country, I had called to let him know it would soon be on sale and in the hands of subscribers. However, there I was almost two weeks later, and the edition was still stuck at the NAHCO shed.

My poor sleeping pattern was worsened by the anxiety. I got up from my office seat, packed my bags and decided to go home. I suddenly became light headed. I thought I was going to faint, but I managed to make it into the car and the driver drove me home. Soni met me at the door, took one look at me, and bundled me into the car. Off we went to see a doctor who carried out series of tests to find out what was wrong with me.

"You're under a lot of pressure and need to take a break," he said before adding, "I would like to keep you overnight for observation."

It was amazing how much of his time Soni sacrificed while I was going through whatever it was I was experiencing.

CHAPTER 5
WHAT HAPPENED TO MY SISTER?

have always loved visiting my sister, Barbara, who live in Watford. She and her husband have a lovely home at Watford junction, and I always have a lovely time when I come visiting. With the doctors insisting I take a break, I decided it was time to let my team run *Genevieve* while I took care of myself. Segun and the rest of the team had always said I didn't have to be as hands-on as I was, which to them meant I didn't trust I had groomed them well enough to run the company in my absence. So, I guess it was time to put them to the test; it was time to put Betty first.

I sensed that my twelve-year-old niece, Sarah, was at the door of my room. She was trying to get in without the door creaking. I sensed her tiptoeing on the carpet, and I knew that the next thing she would do was to take a peep at my face to determine if I was asleep or awake. I turned and said, "Boom!" she jumped and laughed, and then asked the inevitable question.

"Did you sleep, Aunty Betty?" she looked so happy, and I didn't want to burst her bubble.

I smiled. "Yes, I slept...Have you had breakfast, love?" I asked, trying to sway the conversation away from how my night went.

"No, I am going downstairs to have breakfast now. Are you coming?" she asked.

Downstairs in the kitchen, my younger sister, Barbara, was busy with breakfast, the aroma of bacon, eggs, toast and tea, filled the room, but that was a meal I couldn't partake of, as my nutritionist had warned against a certain type of food.

"Hi Betty," my sister greeted chirpily. "Hope you had some sleep," she said, echoing what had become the family's refrain.

She peered into my eyes and saw the answer staring back at her. The lack of sleep was written all over my face.

"Breakfast is ready," she said. "Betty, yours is in the oven." My breakfast was grilled sweet potatoes with tuna and salad. Yummy! Lunch would be whole grain rice, salmon and veggies.

Barbara had taken to fussing over me and making sure whatever it was I was fighting was defeated not a day later. Before I came to England, Barbara hadn't quite understood what was going on.

"Betty, Soni says you haven't been sleeping well," she once said to me.

"Yes," I had answered, "I haven't been able to sleep."

"Ehen, if you don't sleep one night, you will make up for it and sleep the next, abi?" had been her reply. That was how most people saw it, but the reality was different.

For a long while, Barbara hadn't understood what insomnia was. The second week after I got to England, she saw first-hand what I had been unable to explain. Early one morning, she came into my room and saw me sitting up in bed after a night without sleep. She took one look at me, and it visibly frightened her, but she composed herself quickly as she asked softly, "Betty, you didn't sleep at all?"

I shook my head, close to tears, and bit my lips.

"Hmm, it's that bad? I now understand what you and Soni have been talking about."

I think that was truly the first step for her, in understanding what sleep deprivation really was. The next night, she kept watch with me from 9pm. Her husband, Ben, joined us, and we shared some banter. Later, we read the bible and prayed, before they left my room. Barbara brought out a bottle of anointing oil and applied some to my forehead.

Witnessing me go through depression was devastating for Barbara, I could see. From that day, she would fuss and fawn over me. Her children, Sarah and Daniel, would race into my room every morning, greeting me with, "Aunty Betty, did you sleep?" Then, I would get a hug. They already knew what the answer was.

The time I spent with Barbara was very therapeutic for me because she made sure I was never by myself or alone in the room. We would take long walks to Sainsbury's, Asda and Tesco. Barbara has always known that one thing that could cheer me up even at the point of a meltdown was retail therapy. She made time in spite of her hectic catering business, to ensure I got a full dose of shopping, even though I wasn't really interested in buying anything.

One day, after another night of insomnia, I said to Barbara, "Can you book me to see a counsellor?"

She paused, and then said to me, "But Betty, you have seen so many counsellors back home. I think what you need is some time away from all the medications you have taken so far. Let us try a more organic approach to fighting this battle. We will work on your diet, take more evening walks, increase your fluid intake, and try to do the things you have always loved to do. Let us try these things before we consider seeing a counsellor."

A fortnight later, my health had visibly deteriorated and my sister had no choice but to book an appointment for me to see a counsellor. As we drove to the clinic, I recalled when I had gone to see another doctor at LUTH. That visit still leaves a bad taste in my mouth.

What is it about therapists that make you feel worse than you were before a visit? Is it the morose expression they almost always have on their faces, or the way they look like you have intruded into their privacy and cannot wait to show you out?

"What do you do? What is your line of business?" The doctor at LUTH had asked.

On this particular day, LUTH was on strike – what else was new? – and for fear of reprisal, most of the doctors locked their offices. So, I had to be smuggled through the back door to the second floor, where the sleep doctor was consulting. He operated out of a tiny cubicle which offered no privacy, and so everyone in the small waiting room could hear what was going on in the consulting room.

Earlier, as I waited my turn, I had overheard the conversation between the doctor and his patients, and had decided that I wouldn't dare open up the way I would like to. I could hear the entire exchange. This wasn't the case of 'the walls have ears,' it was a case of the ears have no walls. It was free download for everyone. I went in when it was my turn.

"I am a magazine publisher sir," I whispered.
"What is the name of your publication?"
"Genevieve."
"Ah, you own that magazine? My wife would love to meet you."
I sighed.

Once again, he took me through sleep hygiene therapy. And then, like all the others I had seen, he handed me a prescription without any effort at psychotherapy or psychoanalysis.

That night, as prescribed, I took 40mg of Seroxat and went to bed. But hours later, I woke up in a panic. My heart was racing. I was delirious. I woke Soni up, and in desperation, we called the doctor.

"Do you know what time it is?" He asked when he answered the call.

Yes, we knew. It was almost 3am.

"It's my wife, Betty, sir. She is shaking uncontrollably," Soni told him.

The doctor yawned then asked, "The magazine publisher? How many milligrams did she take?"

"40 mg, as you prescribed," Soni said.

"Oh okay, let her reduce that by 20 mg next time. She should have started with 20 not 40 mg," he murmured. "Don't worry, it's just a reaction and she will be fine."

The guy had caused me to overdose on his own prescription yet was annoyed we woke him up? The nerve of this doctor! He said 40mg, and I obeyed. Now, he is saying I should have started with 20mg. Like seriously, it was now my fault?

Barbara and I arrived at the doctors', and again, I was in front of another sullen therapist. She seemed bored and looked at me like 'Oh! Not another one.' She read me many sleep inducing options, most of which every other doctor had already shared with me. It was my turn to look bored. I felt like I had wasted my time again.

Forty-five minutes later, she handed me a prescription.

The morning after seeing the UK therapist, I came out of the shower to see my sister looking curiously at the blister pack of my prescription.

"Betty, you took three capsules?"

"I was trying to sleep," I replied grumpily.

"Betty, the doctor warned you not to take more than a tablet, but you took three."

The therapist had told me to take one pill an hour before going to bed, and I did just that. I took a pill at 9pm, turned off the light and pulled the covers over my head so that the room was pitch dark. I shut my eyes tight but sleep remained elusive. I turned and tossed for over an hour, and then, I decided that one pill couldn't do it so I took one extra. At 3am, after more tossing and turning, I popped one extra pill, but still no joy. I know how I sounded at that particular moment, even to my own self, but hey!

"I was really trying to sleep but the pills were not working," I said to Barbara.

"Betty please, you have to stop trying to overdose. You have to adhere to doctors prescriptions... So, you still didn't sleep?!" I nodded.

She came forward, reached out to me and said, "Don't worry, all this will be over very soon."

"Amen," I responded, and we prayed together.

I made Barbara's home my sanctuary for two months, and she was such a beautiful hostess.

We have always been a close-knit family. Even as kids, my siblings and I had no rivalry among us. It's probably because we learnt very early in life that having one another was all that mattered. We knew early in life what it was like to be caught in the crossfire of a bad divorce. We knew that one parent could pull the plug to your happiness without prior notice, so we always stuck together.

Barbara is my younger sister, the one with the beautiful long hair, the gap tooth... how she loved dancing as a kid. Barbara has always been very caring and multitasking is something she knows how to do best. I have often marvelled at how she ensured that in the process of juggling many balls in the air, none dropped. She is a fantastic and creative cook; she could cook all day. Then one day, she realised that she could make a living from cooking and that was how her catering business was born. You need to taste Barbara's meat pie, and oh, her jollof rice. She gets orders every minute of the day. I remember once eating eight of those meat pies in one sitting, and I didn't feel any remorse afterward.

Gloria is my eldest sister. She is such a brilliant and creative person; she won several laurels for her artistic designs and music talent while she was a student at Queens College, Yaba. She was the one with the straight As. Most of her time at home was spent reading and drawing. It was not surprising that she emerged with First Class Honours in Graphic Arts from Ahmadu Bello University, Zaria, after a distinction in WASSCE. Gloria prays her way through everything, and her faith is one I deeply admire. Gloria, Barbara and

Iye are the family's prayer warriors. They hold up the entire family with their prayer and worship.

Fred, my brother, was such a compassionate, loving and generous child. Although very mischievous, he was the one with the big sense of humour, the family's Mr 'fix it.' Then came Seyi – who we can never refer to as a half-brother because we have never known him as anything but as our brother – he is a six-footer with a teddy bear of a heart, brilliant as they come.

I love my siblings very much, and I am so happy that, in spite of what we went through as young children, the bond was never broken although when each of us eventually opened up, we realised we had carried a lack of forgiveness over the years. We bore marks and scars which hadn't healed, until one day, when we all sat down to talk about how father had hurt us not only because he left, but because of the series of events that followed.

The year after I got married, my father showed up at our place on Webb road, Ikoyi. It was a very awkward attempted reunion. I was sitting in the living room feeding my son, Ruyi. Soni was in the bedroom when the doorbell rang. I got up and looked through the spy hole, and then in shock, I stepped back. I looked again. Yes, it looked like my dad. Mixed emotions rushed through me. I was confused. A part of me was excited, and another part was suddenly rebellious. He rang the bell again, and I hurried into the room as if I had seen an apparition.

"I think my dad is at the door," I told Soni, breathing hard.

"Your dad?" Soni repeated. He looked confused. The doorbell rang again, demanding to be answered, and Soni went to let him in.

I stayed in the room and left the door open a crack so I could see what was going on.

"Welcome, come in sir," Soni said.
He came in and sat in the chair by the window.
"Where is my daughter?"
Oh, how that voice stirred up emotions.
I didn't step out. I waited till Soni came to the room.
"I don't want to talk to him," I said.
"Betty, please just come out."

I followed Soni out and genuflected to greet my father. My traditional manners hadn't left me. He was still my father. Still, I tried to avoid making eye contact. Part of me still loved him. A part of me said he was a good man who made wrong choices. We all make wrong choices at some time in our lives. *But, I wish he had showed up earlier,* I told myself. I had too many questions unanswered, but I had decided they were best left unasked lest the answers raise the ghost of the past again.

Then, there was a pregnant pause. I asked him if he wanted a meal or a drink, he shook his head. I had a million questions to ask, but I didn't have the energy for that conversation right then. The silence was deafening.

At some point, Soni came in and took him to the FRCN club for some refreshments.

It was the last time I would see my father alive. There are so many unanswered questions, and I wish I had seized that opportunity to ask them and set my heart free. Do I regret not making my peace with him when I had the chance to? Yes! Forgiveness is a virtue to the one giving more than to the one receiving.

We never know the extent we would all go in the moments of desperation, in moments when answers are elusive.

Hypnotism!

I never thought a time would come in my life when I would visit a hypnotist in my search of a solution to a health issue that was grieving my soul so much. A long time ago, one of my friends told me about how she went to the Lagos Bar Beach to take a bath on the instructions of her mother-in-law. She had been married a few years, but the children had taken their time in coming. So, her mother-in-law had suggested that she take a bath in the lagoon surrounding the beach.

So, there she was, naked, following the instructions of her mother-in-law. I remember looking at her and thinking, *'Girl, you are well-educated. I can't believe you would allow your mother-in-law talk you into doing such a despicable thing.'* I was full of judgement but she tried to explain she was at that point in her life. She would have done anything to have a child.

When I saw this advert about a hypnotist who could help me restore my sanity I decided I was going to try her. I was that desperate. I knew my sister would object so I didn't let her in on my plan.

"Barbara, I am going to spend the day with a friend. I will be back late," I said.

"Betty, let me take a bath and drop you at the station," Barbara replied. "Who is this your friend?"

"Oh, you don't know her. She's a friend from way back."

I took a train and embarked on a three-hour journey to see this woman with so many testimonies online. I was so expectant and eager to see this hypnotist who would once and for all settle my sleep issues and maybe some of the underlying factors behind this condition of mine.

Her office was in a village. The ambience was serene and the environment was very pastoral, with a lot of trees and greens. It was a small community and everyone knew the other. As she picked me up from the train station, everyone acknowledged her and paid 'homage' to her.

"Let's go for a walk," Rosemary said.

As we walked, she talked to me about her past client. She told me about a man who had never flown in his life because he had a phobia for flying. "In twenty-five years, he never went on a flight, but I cured him of that phobia," she said.

After our walk, we went back to her home/office where she talked about how she had personally benefited from hypnotism.

I couldn't wait. *Bring it on!* My heart screamed. She had a tiny bell in her right hand.

"You are going to fall into a deep sleep," she said. "Betty, just relax. Now, imagine that you have this big blue balloon filled with helium gas. Begin to fill the balloon with every negative thought. Start dumping everything that is negative in your life, wrong association and negative beliefs, start putting everything you have always hated into the balloon. Deposit all toxicity. Fill the balloon with all your anger, hate, unforgiveness, your fears... free yourself. Free your mind!"

Then, she asked, "Have you emptied everything in your mind now? Betty, tie the mouth of the balloon into a knot. Raise it up. Are you ready to let go of the balloon? Okay Betty. At the count of three, LET IT GO BETTY, LET IT GO-O-O!"

"Now Betty, I want you to go back to your childhood. What do you see...? Recall your happy moments... Recall the good times... You are going to start feeling sleepy..." and this went on for a while. Then, I kept thinking to myself, *I can't see anything from my past. I'm not feeling sleepy. Maybe I would soon fall asleep*, I kept pondering.

"You are going to sleep," she said over and over again.

"How are you feeling?" she asked.

"Erm, I'm not feeling sleepy," Instead, my mind was racing. I was focusing so much on that time when the sleep would take me away that I couldn't really relax. Just as I was waiting for that moment when I would go into hypnosis, she said our session was over.

"Hmm, it's different for everyone. Sometimes, you may need more than one session," she said as I stood up. "If it didn't happen now, it will surely happen when you get home and you're in the familiarity of your own bed." As I handed her £300, *I thought, Nah, I ain't coming back.*

For some reasons, as I walked towards my train much later, I couldn't help but find the whole episode with the hypnotist quite hilarious.

At that point, I reflected on what I had read somewhere, about a time when one finds oneself in the belly of the whale. 'In the belly of the whale, desperation meets destination. In the belly of the whale, we experience God more. In the belly of the whale, God turns things around.' I don't know how, but I know for certain that I am coming out of the belly of the whale stronger.

"Welcome back," Barbara said when I got home. "Did you have a good time?"

70

"Yes," I lied.

"Are you okay?" She asked, and I nodded.

My phone rang. It was the hypnotist. I stared at her name on the screen and debated if I should answer it. I decided I wouldn't but would call back in the morning after I had something to report.

I spent the rest of that evening and night wondering if it was entirely her fault or just the fact that I hadn't truly believed that it would work. I was obviously back to where I started. The hypnotist kept calling for updates, but I never answered her calls. I never responded. What was it that made doctors, counsellors, and now a hypnotist say they had helped others and yet left them unable to help me? Did they lack the skills they claimed they had or did they fail to realise the gravity of what I was dealing with? The thought of being the one everyone was unable to help left me wondering if I even knew the gravity of what I was dealing with. I had done what they asked me to do, including giving up work for a while, but what do I have to show for it. I sighed.

Too soon, it was time to return to Lagos, to my family. I had enjoyed my time in the UK, but I knew at some stage, I would have to go back home and begin to focus on getting better. Touch down Lagos, Èkó ò ní bàjẹ́!

Might I add, my G-team surprised me beyond my own expectations. I was so impressed by how they kept the magazine going without me. I felt thankful.

CHAPTER 6
OKAY. IT'S DEPRESSION
🕊

When I was a teen, I loved partying so much that my mom constantly devised ways of curtailing it. While I was between secondary school and University, if I wanted to go to a party on Saturday, I had to tell her by Monday.

"If you can finish doing all these chores by Friday," Iye would say, handing me a long list that included everything from picking Fred from school daily to cooking different dishes during the week.

Sometimes, I would end up going to Sabo market thrice in one week, just to cross off all the chores. I didn't mind though, because the joy and anticipation of going to parties was much greater.

Back then, our party spot was Crazy Horse in Yaba and because our mom was a dressmaker, we were always trendy, the cynosure of eyes. We'd get to a party and dance, sometimes forgetting the 8pm curfew Iye had given us. One day, because it was already 8:30pm, we decided, "Let us enjoy. We'll deal with the punishment when we get home." By the time we got back home that night, Iye had thrown out two pillows for us to sleep with the rats under the stairs.

"Iye, please," we pleaded, knocking repeatedly on the door.

"Iye!"

Eventually, with a few *igbajus*, she let us in.

It was after that we noticed that if Gloria was out with us, Iye would allow us go anywhere and come back anytime. Try convincing our sister the bookworm though.

After we got married, Soni and I socialised a lot because of the nature of his job and mine. It was just another way we fit—we enjoyed the same things. I remember when, in the early years of our marriage, my mother would sometimes come around and she would look at us and say "You people like party sha"

Some days, Soni and I would come home a few times to change outfits to go out. We were always everywhere together, and Iye would jokingly describe us as crabs scurrying around quickly to get from one place to another.

That was how I had always been—social. With *Genevieve* Magazine, it was a no-brainer that I had to attend society events. I enjoyed everything about it, from dressing up in gorgeous outfits to meeting people. So, when I returned to Nigeria after my stay in Watford, I went back to work and all that came with it. However, I soon noticed that I no longer looked forward to events.

It started with avoiding talking to people at events, then wanting to leave early. Eventually, I did not want to attend any social events at all. I just wanted to stay at home, go to work, and lie in bed. Slowly, I was losing my socialisation skills without realising it.

I had not been out to any event in months, and Soni had talked me into attending a wedding with him. One of his friend's sons was the groom. My first instinct was to say, "Ah nah, I will pass. I am not ready for a society wedding and all the paparazzi and the noise."

"It would do you some good," Soni coaxed. "We haven't been out together for a while everyone is always asking after you. Remember how we used to go everywhere together I miss that."

"Hmm... Why not, I said to myself. It's time to stop hiding. I might as well go out to have some fun, I can't seem to remember what fun means anymore, if I want to get better, I would have to learn to face people without feeling any sense of insecurity."

So, I decided to prep for this event. I treated myself to an outfit from Iconic Invanity, booked Johnny the hair stylist, and called in Bayo for my makeup.

As the makeup artist went to work, the more I looked in the mirror and saw my reflection, the more I felt going out wasn't a good idea. The truth is, makeup cannot hide anguish. It cannot hide internal blemish. It cannot mask unhappiness. I decided I wasn't going, but a little voice inside in me said, *Baby steps, Betty. One day at a time.*

I got up, slipped into my lovely dress, and smiled, saying to myself, *You are gonna be just fine*, and off I went to my first outing in a long time.

As I stepped into the reception venue, I was assailed by camera flashes. The paparazzi wouldn't leave me alone, and the thought of my pictures all over the media made me even more nervous and I just froze.

"Aunty Betty?"
"Mrs. Irabor, please look up,"
"We love your dress!"

"We don't understand why every time we want to take your picture you cover your face with a paper or a fan. You are a publisher and you understand how our editors will react when we go back to the office and we don't have pictures of one of the best dressed..., don't do this to your boys."

One of the photographers, whom I recognised from other events, sensed something was wrong and told the others to leave me alone.

He came up to me.
"Are you okay ma?" he asked.

I started to shake my head, but I saw Soni walking towards me and nodded instead.

"Yes, I was just trying to reach my husband."
"I can't go in," I said to Soni when he reached me.

He calmly held me and led me back to the car, and then when I had collected myself, I went in. I would only stay at the party for about an hour before leaving. It was too much dealing with the loud music and the people who wanted to come and say hi.

I dreaded when the pictures would be released but, thankfully, none of those pictures were ever released. This would happen a few more times before photographers started avoiding me at events because they noticed there was a pattern of me trying to hide behind a fan or some other thing that would seem Hollywood-esque, but was just me trying to spare myself some dignity. The few times cameras caught me left me totally sad, as all I saw was the wrinkled face of a woman who was losing it. I didn't see any light at the end of the tunnel. It felt as though I was being gradually eclipsed and I couldn't fight back.

I wasn't out of the woods yet. The battle with insomnia and depression persisted, and my doctor-hopping days were still in full gear. I suppose, in a way, I was looking for someone who really understood what I was going through without writing a prescription even before I finish explaining how I was feeling. That was how I found myself sitting face to face with another doctor in Ikoyi.

My weight was still fluctuating, and the new doctor said it would be a good idea to place me on admission for five nights. Don't ask me what treatment I was getting because I had no idea. The bottom line was that I left the same way I came in and I was four hundred thousand naira short. I had even been conned into buying a special 'insomnia cure' at forty thousand naira.

"This is a special pillow for insomnia," the doctor said, "It's from China. The pillow emits substances that induce sleep." I can't believe I fell for that.

Years later, I smiled when I remembered the forty thousand naira pillow that induces sleep. I got away lucky because he had also tried to sell a special mattress to me at eight hundred thousand naira. Talk about exploiting patients, but I got the chance to give that doctor a piece of my mind.

Shortly before my fifty-fourth birthday, an uncle called and invited me to see a specialist in his clinic. There I was, sitting and waiting when my uncle walked in with the specialist who looked genial.

"Meet Prof," my uncle said. "He's a psychiatrist."

Soni and I glanced at each other. A psychiatrist? Why would my uncle invite a psychiatrist? We couldn't ask questions though as he left us in his office to talk. The psychiatrist took a seat, chatting drily about traffic or some other thing for the first few minutes.

A folder with my name on it lay on the table in front of him. He opened it, was silent for a moment, then asked,

"So, what exactly is going on?"

I took a deep breath to steady myself, but when I tried to speak, I blubbered.

"Why are you crying?" He asked.

"I don't know," I responded as more tears ran down my cheeks. "There must be a reason why you're crying," he persisted.

I looked from him to Soni, back to him and insisted, "I am okay". There was something very gloomy about this guy himself. His words were slow and without emotion.

"Truth is, all I do is cry. I don't seem to need any reason to do that these days," I finally said.

"This has been happening for some time," Soni chipped in.

"Are you sleeping at all?" He asked. It was the worst question you could ask me. Nothing I'd been given to help me sleep had worked.

I shook my head, groping in my bag for wipes or tissue.
"She has seen many doctors, Prof," Soni said.
Then he went on to ask a question no one had asked so far.
"How do you feel about yourself?"

If my tears were trickling before, they started to pour, and I heaved and coughed as I tried to get my words out.

"I'm not happy. I don't know what it is. I'm losing weight and all that," I cried, throwing up my hands in frustration as I failed to find tissue.

He held out a tissue from a box on the table, and as I took it, he said, "Okay. This looks like depression."

Years later, I would bristle about the lack of feeling or explanation that came with his pronouncement, but at that moment, I didn't even raise my head. I felt like I was in a daze and the only thing I could think was, Okay, give me what will make the depression go away.

He wrote a prescription for the first anti-depressant I used, amitriptyline, and said I had to come and see him every two weeks for a start.

I finally had a diagnosis and Soni and I knew what was happening. The past two and half years had been one of the rare times in our marriage when I couldn't talk to him—not because I didn't want to, but because I didn't know what to say to the man with whom I had shared decades and talked with about any and everything. He had just been left wondering, *what is this thing happening to Betty?*

I was a person seeking answers to questions I didn't even know how to frame with words, so how could I find something if I didn't even know what it was? Sometimes, there were shadows of answers. Amitriptyline! I started to sleep after I was put on it by one of my doctors. At first, it was for short intervals, then for hours at a time at night. It gave me an excitement that would have left an outsider thinking, "Is it not just sleep?" It was more than sleep. It was life. It was being able to actually wake up, instead of just getting out of bed tired and weary from a night of forced stillness that kept my body immobile but left my mind racing from worry to anxiety to fear. It was not just sleep. It was being able to taste food again as my appetite gradually returned.

With Amitriptyline, my life gradually regained some meaning. I got up to 6 hours sleep at a stretch and gained some well desired weight. I went from 55kg to 58kg, and then, 60kg, over three and a half years, but I couldn't help worrying about my addiction to Amitriptyline. Every time I tried to wean myself from it, I would plunge back into insomnia. I had found temporary release. The mood swings and depression were on hold as it were. At some point, I even began to worry that I was putting on too much weight, but on the whole, I was on the mend, and that was what mattered at that time. The doctor who placed me on Amitriptyline had warned of its addictive nature, but I was between a rock and a hard place; if I stopped the Amitriptyline I would have plummeted right back into depression, and if I didn't stop, I would have to face the consequences of the side effect and the long term addiction.

When the side effects started, I would weather them, I had told myself. Sleeping and gradually returning to having a calm mind will make it worth it. I was back at work, and not in the zombie way like before. I was back working on articles, conducting interviews and confidently holding meetings with third parties. My mind felt alive! Mental hibernation was over.

So, when my lips started drying, I whipped out my ChapStick more often. Hey, dry mouth? I'll just drink more water! I didn't even care that I had taken to smacking my lips often just to speak. When red blotches appeared on my skin, I simply opted for outfits that covered them. *This sleep and return to normalcy ehn, nothing will stand in its way,* I often thought.

"Mum, do you realise that your face is twitching?" My son Ruyi, said to me one day as we were having a meeting in the office. He was the general manager then.

"What are you talking about?" I couldn't feel anything.

"The left side of your face keeps moving," he said. "It just happened again, but don't worry about it."

When I told the doctor at my next appointment, he confirmed it was one of the side effects of long term use of Amitriptyline and advised that it was time to gradually pull out of it. At this stage, I had weighed my options. I had used Amitriptyline for over two years, and it had given me a temporary relief from insomnia. The bouts of depression were slowly ebbing away, my appetite had returned, and I had added a little weight. Initially, I wasn't sure I was ready to stop the medication just yet, not because of involuntary facial spasm. But, they persisted. Worse still, the potency of the Amitriptyline gradually reduced.

Now, I had no choice but to wean myself from it and try to live a normal life – a life not dependent on antidepressants. The period of withdrawal from Amitriptyline was a bit of a struggle. My body had become accustomed to this medication that it could not function without it, but I kept trying. Surprisingly, a few weeks after stopping Amitriptyline, I went to bed without any sleep aids and woke up around 4am. That was the best I had managed without any sleep aid in years.

I wasn't where I should be, but it was a good start. And, I was learning to celebrate my little baby steps of progress. I even applied the hypnotist's psychological therapy of dumping everything in a balloon and releasing the balloon into space. Every time I felt a negative mood coming up, I would dump everything into the balloon. I would affirm that I was in a good place, that I was getting better, and that I would no longer be in that dark place. I began to try to take control of my mind. This kept me going for months after I had completely pulled myself off Amitriptyline, but soon, I had a relapse.

CHAPTER 7
YOU SHOULD NOT BE SEEN HERE, MADAM

Throughout my battle with depression, nothing humbled me and bruised my ego as much as when I had to go see this next doctor. The Yorùbá have a proverb, '*Tí ìyà nlá bágbé ni ṣọo nlẹ̀, kékèré tún máa gorí'ẹni,*' which means, 'When a big blow knocks you down, smaller ones will come out to play.'

Soni had dressed up to follow me after one of my uncles suggested that we saw a professional therapist at Yaba. I told him not to bother that the driver would take me. My driver, Dominic, had been with me for more than ten years, and he had grown to be so proud that his 'madam' is a top publisher. He basked in the knowledge that I had managed to sustain the magazine over the years. He had been with me since 2003 when *Genevieve* started, and had seen it transform to the brand that it had become. He read every edition voraciously; his favourite columns were 'On the fringes' and 'Morning Dew.'

He had seen me go from one hospital to the other since my battle with depression started, and I realised suddenly he would freak out if he knew which hospital he was taking me to this time.

"Madam, where are we going?"

"Yaba psychiatric hospital," I replied.

"Yaba psychiatric, Madam?!"

"Yes," I said. "I need to go and interview a professor for our mental health edition."

"Ha," his voice piped up. "Why isn't the man coming to the office? Why are you the one going to interview him? Why didn't the editor go?" I didn't respond.

I stared hard at my book, flipping past the page I had been looking for, hoping that the sound would make him leave me to my reading. *If I don't answer, he'll drop it*, I thought. He didn't. As we drove along Third Mainland Bridge, he told me story after story of mentally ill people—"mad people" as he referred to them.

"You should not be seen anywhere near this place, Madam," he persisted as we drove through the hospital gate.

If only you knew, I thought, getting out of the car and walking to the doctor's office.

His office, I would say, was the perfect picture of where you should not take a depressed person. There were piles of dusty books sitting on his table. An old curtain was pulled to the side, revealing bars on a window that looked out to nothing. A sink was in a corner of the room as an old fan droned noisily over my head doing little to keep the Lagos heat away.

"How are you feeling today," he asked. "Can you tell me everything about how you are feeling? I want to know all the medications you have been prescribed. You told me over the phone that it got worse with menopause, please feel free to share everything with me. That is the only way I can help you get better faster."

Once again, as I had done a dozen times, I told him about my journey so far, and my battles. I opened up to him in a way I hadn't done with other doctors. When I finished, I sighed, and so did he. If I had expected something different from all the other doctors, I was disappointed. I am not sure exactly what I wanted to hear, but I didn't exactly get that leap of faith.

Once again, I had a prescription in my hand and several assurances. He smiled as I got up to leave. Sadly, he did not tell me anything to give me hope. How can Nigeria be rated as top on the list of countries with people suffering from mental health issues, yet most psychiatrists and specialists seem clueless? How can they even humanise mental health when they themselves perpetuate the stigma? They make you feel guilty about being depressed.

I told myself I was going to help myself. It seemed suddenly that my recovery was in my hands, and in the hands of the Potter who moulds His clay.

Back in the car, I leaned against the window, grateful that my driver did not try to resume chatting about mad people. I stared out the window as we drove through Yaba traffic, remembering the days of walking through the same streets on my way to or back from school or an errand. As we pulled onto Herbert Macaulay towards the Third Mainland Bridge end, I looked to my left and saw the old Casino Cinema. Well, the relics of it.

I remember the day it was bombed.

The Civil War had been ongoing for a couple of months. Not that I quite knew what a war was at such a young age. We were in Lagos, so life had continued normally for us. On the day it was bombed, July 19, 1967, I was on an errand at Queen Street. I heard a loud sound and saw people running in different directions. I began to race towards the direction of home. As I ran, people asked a woman who had just run into the street what had happened.

"Pomb ni," she said.

As I got home, I saw Mum standing worried at the gate.

"Iye, what was that all about?" I asked, and Mum told me that someone bombed the Casino Cinema. It was then it occurred to me what the woman in the street had meant when she said 'pomb.'

The Casino Cinema at Alagomeji in Yaba was, at the time, one of Lagos's enduring attractions. People went there to watch movies, both foreign and local. It always had posters of famous actors, especially Indian ones, pasted all around it, and adults who could afford it went there for entertainment. On this fateful day, a tanker had been laden with explosives and left in front of the cinema in an attempt by the breakaway Biafran military to strike at the heart of the then capital city. Parts of the casino was destroyed by the explosion, a few people died, and many were injured.

Oh, the futility of war.

"Go on with one Nigeria," I whispered to myself in the car as another relic from the Civil War period dropped in my mind. It was an aphorism coined from using the letters in the name of the then head of state Yakubu Gowon, which also served the intentions of the Federal Government to keep the nation optimistic about its prospects of unity.

By January 1970, when the war ended, Lagos was awash with celebrations and an atmosphere of joy. I remember how all the adults gathered around a radio, listening intently, then burst out in jubilation. "The war is over!"

When I was a young girl, I worried too much. I remember one time I wondered why my mother dismissed suitors so easily considering how much she had given herself to us and carried all our burdens.

I was so relieved when she later remarried someone who doted on us even though we were already in our teens and twenties. We called him Dad. It was nice to see my mother have a second chance at happiness.

Yaba had changed a lot but relics of the past remained everywhere. I suddenly missed those days of wide-eyed innocence when all I worried about was whether Mum would let me go for a party or if I would do well in my exams. Those worries never kept me from sleep though. At the same time, I felt sorry for my younger self. Not out of pity, but just sorry that I hadn't known better what the world is like; that I had made my uneducated assumptions about mental health. I felt sorry for my driver because we lived in a country where no one talked frankly about these things. I wondered how many people were like me—hiding behind excuses so that other people wouldn't know we were having mental health challenges. I felt sorry for the ones who wouldn't even know to get help or how to get help. In the car driving along that day, surrounded by past memories and present realities, I resolved to start writing about my experience. *Maybe it will help at least one person, I thought. If I can just get enough rest to wake my brain.* I longed for the days of being able to sleep deeply. I should have cherished them more.

CHAPTER 8

YOU COULD GO TO JAIL

Sometimes, we pack a bag and think that changing location, jobs, or friends will change our lives. Instead of gathering the pieces and trying to put them back together, we decide it's best we do something new, get a brand new life, as if that will fix what is broken. And maybe it works with some things, but when what is broken is inside us, we just end up carrying it around to the next place. How do you outrun something that is inside you? It presses heavily on your chest, crushing the euphoria of the shopping trip. It churns your stomach till you feel so sick you can no longer even picture the amazing sights you just saw. It screams your worries in your head and they ricochet, reverberating, until you can no longer remember the compliment a stranger paid you that made you laugh and float on air just some minutes ago.

It was early 2012, I decided to take a trip to Dubai and thought while I was there I would also have myself checked out by a therapist. As I began to pack to go for my trip, I felt a new lease of life. Once I started to make plans, buying tickets, protocols and everything else, I felt good, like in the days before I took ill.

Growing up, travelling was a luxury. I remember thinking that when I grow up and can pay my own way, I would travel the world. One day, Mum surprised me with a trip to London. By this time, her business had grown and she had employed over twelve tailors. She had turned our living room in Adébíyí into a factory. She had even bought a car. Demands for her product had tripled and she could hardly meet them. Then came the good times, Mum's effort had paid off. I was in the University of Lagos and there was a strike. The university shut down, and the shutdown was indefinite. Mum said, "Would you like to go to London?" and I screamed, "Yes!"

How I had longed for this moment, especially after Gloria travelled and told us about London.

Then, a flight to London on Nigeria Airways was about two hundred naira, and as students, we got a 50% rebate. I couldn't contain my joy as I stepped into the belly of the aircraft. *I am going to London*. Mum arranged for me to stay at the International Student House at the West End, and that was where I stayed for the period of the school strike, returning only in time for my exams.

After that, my siblings and I also went on a vacation courtesy of Mum, but the mother of all holidays came when my stepdad, Bàbá Sèyí, treated us to a holiday in the UK. He was so extra in giving on that trip. Each of us had a thousand pounds and accommodation at the International Student House. It was sheer luxury. Talk about shopping till you drop. Talk about sightseeing, boat rides on River Thames, and partying. Too soon, the holiday was over.

Even though Dad had given us so much money, he would call to find out if we still had money. We were spoilt silly.

Sadly, many years later, we lost him. But, he remains unforgettable.

My first few nights in Dubai were great. I took my meds and rested. My appetite was not that great; still I explored so many restaurants and ate anything that looked exciting. It wasn't as if I was getting enough sleep, but I was excited about being in the city.

On my fourth day there, I decided it was time to go shopping. I truly enjoy shopping. It was my first time in Dubai, and I had heard so much about the malls. I couldn't wait to just get lost in one of them.

I could shop from 9am to 9pm, seven days a week, and not drop. That was how bad my addiction was. I headed for the mall to pick up a few toiletries. Then, the unbelievable happened at the check-out of the first store I visited.

"Madam, this is a fake hundred-dollar bill." The young male cashier said to me.

"Very funny," I said, and then, I noticed he wasn't smiling. Fear gripped me as my head began to pound.

"Do you have another bill?" It was like the calm before the storm.

With shaking hands and mouth that had suddenly gone dry, I reached for another bill from my wallet. I said a silent prayer as I handed it to him. I watched with dilated pupils as he once again slipped the note under a fluorescent light and shook his head, "This is fake too."

"Ah! *Mo gbé o!* Fake? They can't be," I argued. "I bought them from my bank myself. I signed for them inside the bank!" *Jesus! Jesus! What's going on? What does this mean? Ah, my village people o!* I sighed and waited for his fingers to press the fraud alert button which I was sure was by the till.

Instead, he said, "Madam, I will let you go, but I don't know why I am doing this. You are supposed to go to jail for currency trafficking. This is Dubai."

My heart was racing so fast I thought I was going to pass out and die. Believe me, that was a much preferred option to a jail term. I could just see the headlines back home: ***Genevieve* Publisher, Betty Irabor, jailed for Possession of Fake Dollar Bills.** I could just hear the whispers and the condemnation everywhere, the blogs making me the object of ridicule and memes while my poor children and husband run helter-skelter, negotiating bail for a non-bailable offence like currency trafficking.

"I should go?" I asked. I needed to be sure he didn't mean 'go to jail.' "I should go?" I gesticulated with my hands as I pointed towards the exit doors.

"Yes. Go," he said. I didn't just go. I fled.

I stumbled out of the store clutching my purse. It felt like someone had drained my energy out in seconds. Fake? These were notes I got from a Nigerian bank and they were all fake? The anger that rose in me came as suddenly as the tiredness I had felt only seconds ago. Fake? I was livid.

I got into a taxi and headed home. I knew no peace in the taxi as I kept hearing sirens all the way home. I kept waiting for the taxi driver to get a call asking him to bring me to the station. I saw images of me handcuffed and dragged into a cell where I kept muttering, "I didn't do it. I swear, I didn't do it!" I couldn't stop looking back to see if I was being followed. My imagination was on full activation mode till I got home.

Initially, the bank denied that the currency could be theirs, but when my lawyer presented a copy of the signed document and the serial number of the dollar sold to me, they began to plead and agreed to compensate me. How do you compensate mental trauma? What financial value can any bank place on its fraudulent act? I was ready to press charges, but my lawyer and the bank's counsel agreed to settle out of court.

For a few days, I was scared to step out of the house. I was still affected by the incident at the checkout counter at the mall. By this time, I had arranged an alternative financial arrangement for my holiday. I tried not to allow the incident to rob me off from what was supposed to be a break. Still, I decided it was more important to see a therapist.

As I climbed up the stairs towards the door marked 'Psychiatry,' of a Hospital in Dubai, I couldn't help comparing this hospital with the best of Nigeria's hospitals. *Whatever happened to my beloved country and its health sector?*

Surprisingly, I didn't flinch at the word 'psychiatry.' I was past caring about sitting at a psychiatric hospital. I had no time for vanity, no time for ego claiming. I wanted help, and wherever I could get it was okay. I smiled, thinking, *if my driver could see me now, he would really freak out.*

"Sit down madam," said the psychiatrist as I entered his office. "Madam, how are you feeling?" he asked.

"Not good."

I caught myself staring at him. All he needed was long white snowy beards and he would be Santa. I felt comfortable.

After sharing my recent medical history, he sighed and said, "I can help you, but Madam, from what you tell me, these medicines you've been taking are too many and unnecessary. These medicines are not good for you. What work do you do?"

I looked into my bag and brought out a copy of *Genevieve* and another copy of my book, 'Morning Dew'.

"I am a publisher," I said, turning the pages until I got to the editorial page with my smiling face. My page in the magazine, also called 'Morning Dew,' has always been a favourite of mine, and I happily shared insights about my journey into publishing with him.

He was unbelievably excited. "You are a celebrity?"

"Yes, I am a big celebrity." I sighed, my tone unavoidably sarcastic.

He pointed at my happy face on the book. "This is you. You are very famous." I nodded in reply.

"These are your copies," I said to him, and he smiled then laughed. His excitement was infectious so I smiled too. For a moment, I forgot he was a psychiatrist and I was a patient.

"Madam, magazine is a lot of work," he informed me. "Your medications are too many," he said again, tapping at his table, as he reviewed my bag of meds.

"You don't even need most of them." He started to sort them into two sets and pointed at a set of four. "You can continue with these ones." He pointed at the other set of three, "Throw these ones away. Please, madam."

97

There was something calming about the way he listened to me, answering my questions without making me feel silly. He talked to me like a real person. I had become so used to being talked at by doctors, or, worse still, talked about like I wasn't in the room at all.

"You need a nutritionist to help you design a menu. You need good food and you need liquid, juices and plenty water. You need exercises. All these will help you."

"I've never thought about the lifestyle part," I said to him.

"It's your doctor who should have told you. They should talk to you more instead of feeding you with dangerous pills that will aggravate your health."

"Madam see me again before you go," he said. "Do not worry about your skin. When you start drinking plenty water and sleeping, everything will clear. Trust me madam, I have seen very bad cases, yours is a small case. Don't worry, madam. Pray, madam. Laugh, madam. Laugh!"

"Madam, I won't give you any medicine. Use these ones your other doctors have given you. Go for Hamman, madam. Just relax."

I left his consulting room grinning from ear to ear.

Most of the rest of my two-week Dubai trip was calm, but I was ready to get back home.

Founding and running *Genevieve* stretched me in many ways, especially intellectually. However, it also broadened my experience of other cultures as it often provided travel opportunities. One of such opportunities that I looked forward to was attending Fashion Week in different parts of the world when we could.

My favourite remains New York Fashion Week. Not really because of the fashion week itself—which is superb—but because New York is my favourite fashion city. Away from the main events, I would shop and shop, and even travel to a Neiman Marcus outlet in New Jersey, for their great bargains and discounts on designer items.

In 2011 September, I left Lagos for the Big Apple for yet another fashion week. I didn't go alone this time; I went with a photographer and fashion editor. I was looking forward to representing Nigerian fashion, so I sourced various designs from Nigerian designers. I was going to rock New York City in a way I hadn't done in a long time. I checked into my hotel. Ah! I couldn't wait to hit the fashion scene. I was ready to slay as usual, but that didn't quite happen.

Now, when I tell people I flew to New York for an edition of NYFW but never left my hotel room, their response is the same.

"How?"
"Not even one show?"
"Why?"

From nowhere, the blues hit me. I woke up on my first morning in New York unwilling to face the world. I dragged myself to the bathroom, showered, and as I moisturised and stared at my reflection in the mirror, all of the pigments in my skin seemed to grow before my eyes. I had faced another relapse, sleep had become elusive again.

My beautiful outfits did get worn, and they got compliments each time, but not beyond the hotel restaurant where I walked in and sat to eat each day of my stay. "MD, the show is about to start." My fashion editor would call from the event.

"Okay, I will be there soon," I would say. I was in New York for six days, but not once did I attend any of the shows. They had an idea that the blues were back but said nothing. I had breakfast with them one more time, and while they flew back home, I flew to London and Sonia came to visit. I wasn't sure how much she knew about what was going on with me, but I am sure she saw all the signs. Occasionally, we would talk about it, but I never let her know exactly how bad I felt.

One day, as we got into the taxi to go out in London, she asked, "Mum, you still haven't gone to the health spa outside Kettering?"

She was referring to a spa gift voucher a friend had given me almost a year earlier. It was a great gift idea, but I wasn't sure I was ready for a health retreat just yet.

"No, I haven't."

"I think you should go, mum. A few days at a wellness centre will do you good. Besides, you don't want to waste a gift that was given to you by a good friend."

At her urging, I decided to take advantage of the gift voucher. The journey to Kettering by train was unadventurous. The wellness centre was in Rushton, just outside Kettering. I had called ahead but I wasn't quite sure what to expect.

As the taxi pulled onto the grounds, I took a deep breath. There were fields of green lying ahead, and for some reason, the scenery reminded me of something from *The Sound of Music*. I felt like bursting into song, singing, 'The hills are alive...'

"Ah, Betty we finally get to host you," Suzanne one of the owners of the centre welcomed me. "We have reserved for you one of our best rooms upstairs. We also have a huge surprise for you."

I forced a smile and followed her in. When she led me into my room, I could not help the squeal of delight that escaped my lips. Even I was startled by the sound. It was pink. The surprise was the colour and theme of what was supposed to be my room for the next ten days. Pink. The pillows were fluffed, and the duvet was, *Oh!* So inviting. Small as that gesture was, it cheered me up and made me look forward to the week. From the look of it, they had reserved for me the most luxurious room.

"Have you come from a long journey?" Suzanne asked.

"Yes, New York, London, and now, here I am," I said.

"Okay. Do get some rest and join us for lunch at 2pm," she smiled as she left my room.

I looked at my watch. It was just a little after 11am.

What would I be doing till then? I thought and decided to tuck myself under the fluffed up bed. I began to flip through a copy of *Genevieve* I had been reading on the ride from the train station and that was all I remembered until four hours later when I woke up.

I slept. I slept. I slept.

I hadn't had as much uninterrupted sleep in a whole year. I wiped off saliva from the side of my mouth. I got out of bed. I sang and danced, hurrying to my phone. I needed to share the good news with my family wherever they were on the globe.

"Soni, Soni," I said as my husband picked his phone. "You won't believe, I slept."

"You slept? How many minutes?" He asked.

"Not minutes. I slept for four hours without once waking!" His excitement was palpable, and then I rang my sisters, Barbara in Watford and Gloria in Warri, my brother Fred in Scotland, Şeyi in Maryland, and my mum in Oregun, Ikeja.

"I slept! I slept! I slept!

After I ended the last call, my phone began to beep with messages. They had each called one another.

"Did Betty call you? She slept."

All my family members were so delighted we continued talking about it.

When I suddenly remembered lunch was supposed to have started at 2pm, I showered quickly, brushed my teeth, and raced down to meet the others. 'Others' had finished lunch but decided to sit at table with me after I apologised for falling asleep and rudely being late.

"Where's lunch?" I asked as I stared at the bowl of green soup labelled 'Betty'.

"That's your lunch and, no, it's not the starters," one of the other guests told me with typical English wit.

"But I am very hungry," I complained.

"Well, Queen Elizabeth, welcome to our wellness world."

Having been christened 'Queen Elizabeth' in that moment, it became my name for the rest of my stay.

The next day, my first full day at the centre, I got a better picture of what it offered, and began selecting which activities I would engage in. Most people had come there for detox and weight loss programs, which explained the sparse soups and salads that were a staple at meal times.

Over the days I stayed there, I exercised, got massages, and felt super pampered. My skin even looked better. I particularly loved the Nordic walks. The first time I tried it, I thought it was weird because we walked using these things that looked like ski poles. The goal was to involve the entire body in the walking process. Once I got used to it though, the open air and lush fields made me long for longer walks. I did not even mind the September cold.

By the fifth day at the centre, I felt energised, especially after series of detoxes and colonics. Unfortunately I didn't have the luxury of sleeping for hours for the rest of my stay. The most I got was an hour or two at a stretch. I made up for it by lying in bed for stretches between activities. Sometimes, I'd read pages of my copy of 'Battlefield of the Mind' by Joyce Meyer. I had been carrying it around for months since a friend gave it to me. Other times I'd just lie still, mindfully breathing deeply and exhaling.

One day, Suzanne told me I could see a hypnotherapist.

I responded with a loud *No way!* It was so loud we both burst out laughing. I was having so much fun there that I began to dread going back to the real world. It was the first place I had slept deeply in a long time. The whole environment lifted my spirit.

When the time came to leave, as I embraced everyone who had been my family for ten days, Suzanne said to me, "Betty, don't give in to depression, you have got to fight it."

I nodded.

"You're different from that woman who came in. You're looking a lot better than when you arrived," she said. I knew it was true, and I was not surprised when she confessed that when I arrived she had thought I had a terminal ailment. I had dropped down to a size 2 at the time.

I was going to miss it all; the Nordic walking, the soups, the camaraderie. At the entrance with my bag, ready to leave, I hugged my new friends in turn. They had been so jolly good to me. They had shown me love and care. They had given me so many reasons why I should fight depression. They had shared their stories of grief with me.

I left there with many nature-based meds. I had noticed how the combination of detox, exercise, and even simple things like starting the day with a drink of warm water with lemon and lime, had helped my bowels. I was hopeful that continuing those practices would help, yet I was filled with trepidation. It was part of the lifestyle changes the doctor had suggested to me in Dubai.

My friend, who had gifted me the voucher, was right when she said, "I promise you will feel much better after you have spent some time in this place." Deep down inside of me, I felt an awakening coming through. I was ready to begin the fight to claim back what was mine.

CHAPTER 9
DUST TO DUST

I cannot remember when exactly I discovered the power of words, but I know it came long before I knew the power of having a platform and how to combine both. I do remember clearly two incidents that showed that being a journalist gave me a power I could use for good or evil, and helped me shape the type of stories I wanted to tell. I went from writing just as a way to deal with my own thoughts and personal outlook, to thinking about the potential good I could do through my writing.

Shortly after I left National Concord where I cut my teeth in journalism, I began freelancing for a number of newspapers. One of my early articles was about an airline's nasty treatment of Nigerians. The airline was always described as racist but I got to experience that first hand on a flight to Lagos, which by the way is their most lucrative route, ever. How dare they bite the hands that feed them?

A new mum, who ought to have been seated in one of the front seats, had been assigned a seat way back by the toilet. She complained that she had specifically asked for the seats usually reserved for new mums and their babies, but the male attendant snubbed her even as she tried to quieten her infant. When she politely asked the flight attendant to move her to the right seat before take-off, especially as it was unoccupied, the attendant pointed towards the aircraft door and said, "Madam, if you don't like your seat, you may still get out." Then, under his breath, he muttered, "You and your people are such a handful."

At the same time, a passenger had requested for a pain killer and water, and another attendant had retorted, "We have run out as it seems everyone on this flight boarded with a headache." At that, she and her other colleagues chuckled! In that moment, I felt so furious and decided I was going to get a million signatures calling for sanction against this airline. I pitched the article to The Guardian Nigeria newspaper, and after it was published, two managers of the airline flew in to Lagos to meet with me. They apologised on behalf of the airline and offered me a business class round trip ticket to a destination of my choice. I turned down the offer and insisted on getting a million signatures to have the airline sanctioned or banned. When they could not cajole me into backing down, they then sent a top lawyer to do the job. First, he threatened me, and when that didn't work, he hinted at a gift in a 'brown envelope,' which further infuriated me. Then came the pressure from all quarters until I yielded. At this stage, Nigerians were clamouring to sign my petition.

While the airline incident was from my standpoint as an onlooker, the second article was about one of the most painful incidents of my life. In 1991, I found out I was pregnant. I was going to be a mum again. Sonia was just two at the time, while Ruyi had finally settled into his 'big brother' role. I went to my uncle's hospital for a check-up, and with a somewhat creased brow, he instructed me to go have a scan at a well-regarded hospital in central Lagos.

"They have a scanning machine, so I want you to go there," he said.

I had given birth to both Ruyi and Sonia at Osagie Medical Centre (OMC), attending all my pre- and antenatal appointments there. OMC was home to me. It was run by my late uncle and the nurses and doctors were family.

So, on this fateful day in 1991, I went off to another hospital to have a scan.

"I am here for a scan," I told the receptionist as I handed her my note from my doctor.

"Sit down," the receptionist said while she went to fetch the 'scan lady.'

"Follow me." I looked up as a lady in a green hospital uniform beckoned.

She obviously wasn't one for small talk, I thought, as I followed her instructions. She didn't have time for a smile either, but I was too happy to care; I was going to have baby number three! That was all that mattered.

Much later, after the scan was done, the scan lady glanced at me and said, "Is this your first pregnancy?"

I smiled, "No, this is my third."

"So, how come you didn't know that the baby was no longer moving and that it might have died?"

"What did you say?" I asked tearfully. She was joking, right?

There were too many things happening at once for me to process. My baby had died? There wasn't going to be a baby?

"Get up and dress," she said coldly, "I have other people waiting for a scan."

That was it? Is this woman human at all? I wondered as I freely shed tears all the way back home. I didn't know that I could be affected by something that wasn't really tangible yet.

I went into the hospital for an evacuation, which is just a surgery to get the baby out. It is just one of those experiences that one must put behind one no matter how difficult.

But I had a duty to ensure that the hospital where I had the scan was called to accountability. They shouldn't be let go without being cautioned. That "scan lady" needed to be called to order. I called out the nurse and the hospital in my column, "Candy floss," at *Classique Magazine*; published by my dear friend, late May Ellen Ezekiel, popularly known as MEE. Ranking as one of the pioneers of lifestyle publishing, she was the one who got many of my peers interested in publishing, because of her powerful pen. I will never forget her piece on 'Over Cognac,' where she lamented how people she called her friends had assassinated her character over a drink of cognac! And then there was 'Pilgrim Souls.' Ah, May was the pen idol of that time.

Following the publication of my story on the scan lady, there was an uproar by readers who asked that the erring nurse be disciplined while the hospital tendered an unreserved apology to me. Knowing that another woman out there was potentially being spared such an awful experience gave me some measure of comfort. As for the nurse, I couldn't be bothered about her. I was over her.

With *Genevieve*, I truly came into a place where I was able to tell important stories, amplifying experiences that were otherwise swept under the rug in our society. Each edition left me feeling like I had fulfilled my purpose in greater measure—that was until depression stole that from me and replaced it with thoughts of worthlessness. It was no surprise then, that when the most shattering event of the last decade happened to me; I had no words to say. I had no words to write. I had no way to process my feelings and thoughts fully until I started to write this book.

On September 4, 2012, I got a phone call from my young cousin who lived with my mum and my brother Fred who had just moved back to Nigeria.

"Fred is ill, aunty," he said.

I found out he was on admission at a Government hospital in Ikeja. Since returning from my trip to Kettering a year before, I had continued many of the practices I learnt there and even though I still was not getting many hours of sleep, I had improved so significantly that I had returned to immersing myself in work and even attending the odd social event. On that day, I had committed to attending a book launch and was running late, so I asked Soni, "Should I go to the book launch first and then head to Ikeja, or go to see Fred first?"

"No, go to the hospital first. Family first," he said.

I walked into the hospital ward and saw my brother's frail body lying in bed. As soon as he saw me, his eyes lit up somewhat. We had been on the journey together from when he was a baby battling with sickle cell crises. From the time we moved to Yaba, I would join my mum as we made the long journey to LUTH in Idi Araba. The crises mostly started after midnight, but Iye would wake me up around 1am if it was not abating.

"Betty, wake up. Fred needs to go to the hospital."

Those words cleared my eyes faster than anything. Even when we lived in the barracks, I had often been the one to take care of Fred, so we had a bond that was probably deeper than that of a regular filial love among siblings.

We had no car in the first few years of living with Iye, and we could not afford private hospitals that were closer to our house, so we would walk a considerable distance down the length of Herbert

Macaulay Way before a rickety cab would pull up by us and take us the rest of the way to LUTH.

The walk would start with Mum carrying Fred, then when she got tired, I would carry him. We would alternate on the long walk from Akínwùnmí—later from Adébíyí Street to which we moved—to Herbert Macaulay near Kakadu and Singer Machine. We could be there for an hour or more before we would find a taxi driver who was willing to accept whatever rate Iye had haggled.

At LUTH, there would be another wait even as Fred writhed in pain and we watched on helplessly. We'd get to the hospital and sometimes there would be no doctor for three hours. He'd groan, holding on to his tiny legs, while all we could say was, *"Pèlé. Sorry."*

We did that for several years. I didn't understand what was happening, but I was always filled with a fear I could not express in words or even tears. The nurses were often curt and he wouldn't get any relief to tide him over till the doctor arrived. It was my first experience of pain up close.

One night at the hospital, we met a doctor. I'd later find out it was Professor Olíkóyè Ransome-Kúti, and he had experience with child health care. He instructed the nurses that, on future visits, they were to call him in his quarters instead of keeping us waiting till the morning. Iye and I got a bit of a break after that. We'd get to the hospital and he'd be there. Sometimes we'd call him on the landline and he'd pick and tell us what to do.

As he grew older, the crises abated significantly.

Fred looked seriously ill that September morning when I saw him at the hospital. My first instinct was to move him to Royal Cross Hospital in Obalende, where he had received treatments in the past, but the doctor assured me that he was responding to treatment.

Worried because of my own recent experience of feeling like I was an experiment in the hands of the doctors I had seen for depression, I pressed the doctor for more updates on his current situation.

"Are you sure I shouldn't move him?" I asked again. "He looks delirious."

"Don't worry, madam," he insisted. "It is because of the sedatives we gave him. Once he falls asleep and wakes up, he will be much better." I relaxed somewhat after that, and felt confident enough to go to the book launch in Victoria Island. I moved closer to Fred and hugged him.

"Fred, I need to quickly go somewhere, but I will be back, okay?"

He attempted a smile and nodded slightly. I squeezed his hand and promised to come back with some Chinese. Then, I dashed off. I was impatient through the event, and once it ended around 2pm, I did not wait to network as I usually would. On the way back to the hospital, I told my driver to stop by a Chinese restaurant so I could buy some—it was Fred's favourite. When I got back into the car and picked my phone, I had over twenty missed calls, and before I could check for the list of callers, my phone rang.

"MD, where are you?" One of my staff members asked as soon as I picked his call.

"What do you mean?" I replied. "Where are you?"

He said he was at the hospital with Fred, and just wanted to know where I was. As we talked, my phone continued to beep from waiting calls.

"I'm on my way to the hospital" I said to another caller.

"MD, don't bother. Fred will be discharged soon."

That's strange, I thought.

"I am already on Third Mainland Bridge, so there is no point turning back."

"MD, you can turn back before Oworonshoki. Fred is alright now."

"I'm coming," I insisted. "Tell my cousin to wait for me. I bought Chinese food for Fred." As I got out of the car at the hospital, I saw my *Genevieve* team.

"Why are you all here? I asked. "You all didn't have to leave the office to come see Fred, I hear he will be discharged soon. Who even told you people that Fred was ill?" For the first time I looked at them. Their smiles were odd, and they seemed to be avoiding direct eye contact with me.

"Where is Fred?" I began to panic. There was no coherent answer. Someone said he was in the Intensive Care Unit while another said he was getting ready to be discharged.

"Okay, where is my cousin, Idahosa?"

Idahosa and Fred were close beyond being cousins. I was certain things would make sense if Idahosa explained. I sat in the car and waited since there was no one to point me to where Fred was. Idahosa did not pick his calls but he finally showed up about an hour and half later. My staff members rushed to his side whispering as soon as they saw him. I stepped out of the car.

"Why did you phone to tell them Fred is in the hospital?" I asked. He was quiet. He had his baseball cap pulled over his eyes so I couldn't see his face clearly.

"Where is Fred, Idahosa?" I was getting irritated.

"When I'm talking to you, remove your cap," I said impatiently, snatching off the baseball cap from his head. Then, I noticed he had been crying, and immediately, I saw his puffy red eyes, I screamed at him.

"Are you deaf? Idahosa, I said where is Fred?"

"I... I... Imetin tae," he replied. Idahosa had a stammer, but it was more pronounced than usual as he said to me in Bini, "It is too heavy for me to say."

"U imetin tae?" I asked.

"Fred wu." Fred is dead.

"Fred wu?!" I screamed. "Hoooooow?! Fred wu?"

I crumbled to the ground, unable to hold myself up as the weight of the news of my brother's death fell on me. My staff tried to hold me up. I don't even know how we got to the front of the Intensive Care Unit in which they had claimed he was, but I felt in that moment, that I would die. That I ought to die and just end the sorrows life seemed to be meting out to me daily. I rolled. I curled. I beat my thighs and howled as my staff whispered, "MD, please take it easy. People are looking."

I didn't care. I sat on the stairs leading to the ICU and howled my pain, at some point digging my nails into my skin. Yet, in all of that, I could not find tears. They just would not come.

A while later, I saw attendants wheeling what was clearly a body out. I lunged at the mortuary attendants.

"Fred is in there. Fred is in there," I said, reaching my hand out as Idahosa and someone else held me back. I wanted to see his face, to see his body, to see my baby brother one last time...

My heart broke for my brother, dead at forty-nine, but my heart also broke for my mother, a woman who already knew too well life's sorrows and losses. Soni, who had been stuck in traffic hoping to make it to the hospital before I got there, finally arrived, but no measure of comfort can fix some things.

I started calling my siblings.

"Gloria, Fred is dead."

"Barbara, Fred *tiku*."

"Seyi, we lost Fred."

I kept the conversations brief as each started to ask questions. "Why? What? How? When?" Everyone was plunged into mourning. We had all been part of Fred's sickle cell journey. I think the worst part was that we had all seen him go through even worse bouts of the crisis. We didn't expect that this one would be his last. Telling Iye was the hardest part. Two days after Fred's death, we still hadn't found a way to tell her.

She'd ask about him, and we'd give an excuse.

"Betty, I haven't heard from Fred since Idahosa took him to the hospital," she called me the day after.

"Oh, he's getting better. I moved him to another hospital," I lied.

"I tried to call Idahosa, but he's not picking. I tried to call Fred but his phone is off."

I would say to her, "Iye, don't worry. I will get Fred to talk to you later."

Indeed, Fred's phone was off. It wasn't death alone that 'off-d' his phone it was a hospital thief. The minute he died, someone on the hospital staff had stolen his phone and his watch so that we could not even reach his friends to inform them of his demise. All my siblings came to Lagos, and we eventually broke the news to Iye. Don't ask me how she took it; it is better imagined than spoken. But I will never forget that SCREAM. I ran upstairs as everyone else tried to calm her. But then Iye was never one to stay down and broken for longer than necessary. Her faith is that strong.

When Fred died, I could not find my words and I could not find my tears. Even after, I wondered if he would have had a chance to survive were he not in a Nigerian hospital. Idahosa told us how he had been left on the floor at the hospital for a while because there was no bed, and when he had finally paid one of the nurses, a bed was suddenly found. I remembered again, all those years he would hold his legs as a child in LUTH, while we waited to see a doctor, and it cut deep that over forty years later, the same situation had eventually taken his life. Dust to dust.

CHAPTER 10
DUST CHOKES

Whatever I had gained from the changes at the wellness centre were quickly lost as I plunged in again, leaving nights spent replaying my brother's death alongside the other events of the last few years.

I spent months being 'strong,' but I also knew each day was bringing me closer to a breaking point. When my friends asked, and it was often, "How are you, Betty?" I either avoided answering or pretended all was well. Soon, the former became my go-to, until I barely talked with any friends. With everything happening in my life, I had come to realise that there were many people – friendships and relationships – I needed to edit out of my life, and the only way I could think of doing it was the way the hypnotist had suggested. I put each of them in a blue helium balloon, knotted it and let it go. Right now, some friendships are somewhere in space, floating in a blue helium balloon. Ah!

A few friends remained with me through this journey, one of them was Barbara Lawrence; she was supportive through the difficult times. I met Barbara while she was a columnist at Vanguard Newspaper. I was a feature writer at National Concord, but I really enjoyed reading her column, Fashion Fair. Even before I met her, I knew I liked her, so whenever I saw her at events, I made it a point to chat a little. Then, we became very good friends turned sisters. She became a family member, and when Sonia was born, she became her godmother. Like all my siblings, Barbara has always been there for me, but she was one of the first casualties of my state of health. I remember one of our big fights one day she made a comment that I considered inappropriate. As always we made up soon after but she was always at the receiving end of my moods.

On my fifty-sixth birthday, I said to the security guard at home, "If anyone passes through this gate, you've lost your job."

I was not ready to entertain anyone; I had not left the house in days. Every time I heard the toot of a horn at the gate, I would stand at my bedroom window and peep out the barely drawn curtains to see people dropping cakes and gifts when he refused them entry. But, Barbara came and wouldn't let my gateman deter her. I had no choice but to let her in.

"You'll come in, but you won't ask questions, deal?"
"Deal."

I came downstairs. We spent the day together, talking about everything but my health. She did not try to choke rational positive talk down my throat. That, however, is not to say that Barbara and I hadn't had some heavy collisions in the early years of my ill health when she didn't know what was going on with me. Now, we laugh over those days because, in retrospect, some of them were so weird we are glad we can now find humour in it. I remember the day she made an off remark at her niece's wedding, and I ran out of the wedding reception with her in hot pursuit, until we both became breathless.

Twenty children cannot play for twenty years, goes a Yorùbá proverb, but many of my friends and I had, before depression made an incursion, kept our friendship going for as many years or more. In the midst of the storm though, blinded by all the dust events had raised, I forgot how much strength I had drawn from friends like Alero Roberts, Joke Silva, Ifeoma Anyigbo, and a few others.

Following Fred's death, I began to replay my life with him, especially the various hospital visits during his crises. I also played back the years when we had all been so far apart geographically, but I could still dial a number and hear his voice on the other end.

On the one-year anniversary of Fred's death, I plunged further into the black hole. Memories of his lost battle with sickle cell kept replaying in my mind while I was sitting in church until I couldn't hold it together. I left the church and hurried down to the hospital to see my doctor. I feared I was having another melt down. The hospital wasn't far from the church so it was a quick drive. I needed badly to drown the negative voice in my head.

"How are you dear?" Soni asked as he walked into our bedroom. "Are you feeling better?"

I grunted. He sat on the bed and touched my cheek.

"Ah, can I switch on the lights? It's a bit dark here. See, I got you some cheesecake."

"Hello Soni. You can turn on the light," I smiled, "and yes I would like a slice of the cheesecake." Everyone in my family knew how much I love my cheesecake. I once finished an eight-inch cheesecake in one day and felt sick after.

"You have to come out from under the duvet to get it," Soni said.

I threw the duvet to the side and got out of bed on wobbly legs. I was tired and groggy from meds.

"Have you had your bath at all?" Soni asked. When I shook my head, he said, "Let me run a bath for you, it will do you some good."

As I walked into the bathroom, I knew it would take more than a bath to fix me. It would require a Jesus-type miracle from the look of things. It had been five years since I started dealing with depression, yet, each day still made me think, *how did I get here?* It was getting harder and harder to remember life without the feeling of being blinded and choked by dust.

"Betty, are you okay? Your cheesecake awaits o," Soni called out.

"I am coming," I said, towelling myself on my way out of the bathroom. I felt a bit nauseous and sick. On the bed, I ate my cheesecake, slowly fighting a wave of melancholia as Soni watched.

"Are you okay?" He asked

Poor guy, it had not been easy for him. I may have been the one going through the bout of depression but he suffered just as much. He always appeared strong, but I could see it in his eyes; he was worried sick.

Three weeks earlier, I had done the unthinkable and tried to overdose on my anti-depressants. The urge was too strong and it seemed like the perfect way out of years of misery. It wasn't something I planned. It had just engulfed me that Sunday morning until it was all I could think about: *taking my life.*

Suddenly, my heart began to beat faster, and I began to pace up and down the room.

I glanced at the corner of the room and suddenly, I couldn't wait. I raced to my dressing table, which was like a pharmacy, picked up a bottle of antidepressants, and dashed into the bathroom.

Soni raced after me and wedged the door with one foot screaming, "Betty, open the door! My leg! My leg!" Eventually, he managed to push the door open and caught up with me just as I tried to empty the bottle of medicine in my mouth.

From then on, Soni would say to me, "Don't lock the bathroom door," whenever I headed to the bathroom.

"Betty, are you okay?" He'd call out every few minutes if I was in the bathroom and he could not hear any activity.

I thought about how much his business had been affected by our constant trips to the hospital. Besides the one-off visits, whenever I had been admitted, he would come to spend some hours with me each day, waving away my protests for him to leave after spending a few minutes.

He wasn't the only one. Ruyi had completed his Master's in Film Directing and moved back home. He ensured he spent more time with me, sharing series of affirmations and inspirational quotes with me. We would talk about 'The Secret,' and how we could win battles with our mind sets.

As much as possible, we had down played what was going on and my mum didn't really see the whole picture. She knew I was not in the best of health but she didn't know half the story. She would often complain that I had lost weight and should eat some more. One day, she came bearing 'Wate On,' to help me add some weight. Mum thought I was on a diet and would reprimand me. I could tell she was worried that I stayed in bed too often. This wasn't the same daughter she often called a crab because I couldn't sit still. She called Soni and I crabs, she said we partied a lot.

Mum spent most of her time praying for her children, especially me. I'd walk in to see her binding and casting out Satan. My siblings, Gloria, Barbara and Ṣeyi, were not left out of the prayer marathon.

Everybody was on bended knees. Gloria went the extra mile and would send me herbs– organic, fresh powdered Chamomile tea which she would order from Senegal.

Love and affection were things I didn't lack, but no matter how much you are loved, it cannot take away some things. In fact, in those days, it was often hard to see or accept that love. I was more inclined to feeling like I was a burden on them all. They could be spending their time and money on better things than praying for me and trying to find solutions to something that now seemed like it was determined to dog me the rest of my life.

There are days in 2014 that remain imprinted in my memory because they were days of depths I had not thought it possible for a person to sink to. On one such day, while on admission, Soni invited a priest to administer the sacrament of the Holy Eucharist. I happily received the Holy Communion but thought, "Could this be the last sacrament I ever receive?"

He never told me why he invited the priest, but considering that my physical body had weakened so much that I sometimes collapsed when trying to stand, he probably thought I was on my way out of this world.

I would take this tablet and that one, yet the more I took, the sicker I got. I looked for help in places I would never have agreed to previously. One of such was some dingy hospital. Walking in and being greeted by the old wall paint and rusty chairs in the reception,

I knew the hospital hadn't seen any renovations since the seventies. It was the type of place to which you'd ask someone to bring you a bucket from home.

"I need to admit you and examine you for a few days," the doctor insisted. "We may need to feed you intravenously too."

I took one look around his office—no better than the reception that had made me want to keep my body or bag from touching anything. I sighed, glanced at Soni, and shrugged.

"I've come this far," was all I said.

From our chat, the doctor seemed to know a little more about insomnia-induced depression than the other doctors I had seen so far. Also, unlike the others, he listened and let me speak without interrupting my flow. I opened up to him about the past few years and how nothing had seemed to work. He empathised with me, and after my session, he prescribed three new types of medication. I wasn't comfortable with the cocktail of drugs but he assured me they would help me sleep.

So, I spent a night lying on a thin mattress on a bed in his clinic. When a nurse tiptoed into my ward around 1 am, she was shocked to see me awake. She called the doctor to give him a report, and he told her to administer an injection. It was at this point I refused.

"I already took three tablets you prescribed a few hours ago," I protested. As with the others, I suddenly felt like a lab rat, like there was a lot of trial and error going on. I called Soni to complain, and he agreed that I should not allow any injection if I felt that way.

The next night, I broke down and moaned, "I want my life back. I just want my life back."

That night was made worse by some peeping toms.

"Are you Betty Irabor, the magazine lady?" A nurse on night duty asked as she walked shyly into my room bearing a tray.

This is no time to be Betty Irabor, I thought and managed a smile.

The next morning, with all the strength left in me, I told Soni it was time to go home.

"If you don't discharge me now, I'm going to discharge myself," I told the neuropsychologist.

"She's going to do it," Soni chipped in.

I was discharged, and we went home.

But, this last hospital visit left me with a memory that I will not forget in a hurry. This was another case of wrongful prescription. It was a tiny pink tablet, but my system was repelled by it. While it remained in my system, it did all the harm it could. I had followed the last doctor's instructions and swallowed the pink pill after dinner. And then, I began to react. I couldn't sit still, my heartbeat increased and so did the palpitations, until I wondered if I was having a fit.

My son and my husband rallied around me, and Soni hastily dialled the doctor's number. I could hear him describing the last medication I took.

"Just right now, after dinner," Soni said.

I got up like one in a daze and got a pen and piece of paper scribbling down instructions. With all the strength I had left in me, I began to update my will. I kept scribbling as everyone gathered around me. My strength was failing me, and that day, I was ready to let go.

"What are you writing?" Soni asked when he got off the phone.

I just kept scribbling without responding to anyone. My body jerked involuntarily, and my mouth and throat were dry. I was blacking out as I kept hearing my name.

"Betty. Betty!"

I scribbled until I had listed most of the things I wanted to leave for everyone. I tried to remember the combination to my safe where my jewellery and documents were. It took a while but I cracked it. I included it in my last note.

"Betty," Soni said. "The doctor said we should come to the hospital immediately."

I refused.

The doctor eventually recommended glucose, and someone rushed out into the night to get it. Gradually, the effect of the medication began to wear off, and I became calm again.

DEW

CHAPTER 11

WHEN THE DUST SETTLES

They say it's always darkest before the dawn, and those words proved true in my battle with depression. Everything I had tried had not worked, so I gave up on my body and mind. I was just going through the motions daily. If I could, I went to work. If I couldn't, I stayed home under the duvet with the heavy curtains pulled to keep out light as much as possible.

One day, Soni came home. He seemed very excited; he had listened to a therapist on a radio program, and he told me that he liked her approach to depression and mental health. He spoke so highly of her and urged me to go see her, at least for what it was worth.

"Nah," I said. "I am tired of doctors, psychiatrists and therapists. No way! I am tired of doctors who want to fast track and jump start my recovery through pills."

They just want to sit, pretend to listen, talk at me in a condescending, judgmental tone, and get their cheques.

Soni persisted, so I decided to humour him by going to see this doctor.

I did not expect that I would walk into her office and my first session with her would last nearly three hours, just talking. Me talking and she listening.

I went in, the picture of nonchalance. As I sat across from her, the first thing I noticed was her friendly face. I didn't shed my attitude though. *What will she tell me that I haven't heard before? I* thought. I was eager to get to the end and collect the prescription I was so sure I would be hit with, so that I could go home and tell Soni I had tried.

However, there I sat for three hours, and this lady barely wrote anything in that time. I was confused, at first. I was so used to doctors who barely glanced at me because they spent most of the time scribbling on white sheets that were held to my folder by twine or an office clip. I paused in the middle of answering a question, wondering if I should ask her if she didn't want to take notes.

"Go on," she said.

It was clear she was listening. In the middle of answering a question of hers, she would sometimes ask me to pause, and then she'd raise something I'd said earlier and ask if it was connected in any way to what I was saying at the moment.

This was new for me. She seemed to not only have all the time in the world for me, she was listening and barely talking. She'd take me back to what I'd said. She was more interested in how to wean me off the meds. If anyone had asked me if there was something that would make me feel like a weight had been lifted off me, I wouldn't have thought it was talk therapy. As she asked questions and I answered, pouring out my thoughts and feelings without being cut short and judged felt like a deep exhaling.

"Next time, when you're coming, come with a list of all the medications you've taken over the past few years," she said as I told her about some of my experiences with meds and doctors.

Sometimes, we don't realise just how much we have burdened ourselves with, and how those burdens then try to take over our lives and choke us. By my third session with Naya Ndupu, I was getting more comfortable with her.

There were things that had grown from seeds I didn't even know had been planted over the years. However, sitting across from Dr. Ndupu and guided by her questions, I began to realise just how many negative seeds had taken root in me, and how I had developed coping mechanisms that made me seem okay for the most part, but had failed to deal with the root issues. Some things—like my negative image of self—had to first be uprooted before other things could take root. Sometimes you just feel like you're overreacting because other people have gone through worse.

Menopause and its attendant hormonal upheaval had acted like a whirlwind that raised dust I hadn't even known was in my life. This was why I had choked for many years and stumbled around blindly, groping for light even as I felt like I was being buried alive. As Dr. Ndupu helped me to realise what was the whirlwind and what was the dust, we were able to begin the process of settling the dust.

She worked with my body, mind and emotions; she listened to it all, seeking to know how one affected the other. She had a plan and was consistent. Whenever she prescribed medication, she was quick to take me off it if I started to experience side effects. She was comforting in telling me the ones that would pass after a few weeks. If I needed to refill a prescription, she wanted to talk about it first to be sure I truly needed it and it was working. She was more interested in weaning me off meds than pumping me with them. She was far from the nodding, dismissive doctors.

Sometimes, she would call to check on me, or listen at odd hours as I shared fears or asked questions.

In all this, we never talked about me being Betty—something that had started to feel like a curse by that time. It was only later I knew she knew who I was. I was glad for it—it had allowed me the comfort of vulnerability without worry or the irritation that had accompanied some others making reference to who I was.

With Dr. Ndupu, I was relieved, although a part of me kept waiting for the other shoe to drop. It had to be too good to be true. All these years and there seemed to be something working? It had to be too good to be true.

But, it wasn't. We were partners in my recovery. We were always interfacing, finding solutions together, looking at the underlying factors, and deciding which new coping skills or treatment courses I needed. It was like someone was holding my hand and leading me through a tunnel in which I hadn't been able to see or even grope my way along to light.

It was from her I learnt that most people have things that trigger certain behaviours in them, so I started learning to recognise mine. Regardless of the menopausal hormones that had blown things up, I had to learn the other triggers I had—like replaying the past instead of letting go—so that I could learn to deal with them, instead of hoping I wouldn't be subject to life changing or body altering events anymore.

⌄

As I wrote in my study and played Nicole C. Mullen's 'My Redeemer Lives', I got curious about the lyrics and Googled them. I picked up the Bible and read from the book of Job from where some of the lyrics had been taken. *Poor Job, he actually went through all this and survived? He was worth dedicating 42 chapters to in the Bible. But Job was a man, he was in the Bible.* He had conversations with God, but I am a woman and I am not a Biblical character. I was in this tunnel that has no end and I wish I had one hundredth of Job's faith and grace. Before those trials began, God knew Job would win, just like He knew I would overcome mine.

I suddenly understood Isaiah 43:1-7 and why God is empathetic. I realised the fire didn't burn me. Everything I was going through was because He knew I had the capacity and it couldn't destroy me.

Through it all, someone, something came just in time, and I was able to shed decades of burdens I hadn't even known I was carrying.

As I began to take steps towards light, I also began to retrace my steps towards God. I realised that for a while, I had stopped talking to Him because I felt He had not been there for me. I had wanted a miracle; I had wanted depression to evaporate. And, in truth, I had read and heard many times over the years that if one prayed enough and had faith enough, such things could go, just like that.

However, as I took each step in the recovery journey, I also learnt that God was more interested in this. Interested in my learning what was wrong, unlearning maladaptive behaviours, and learning how to live as a whole person. That was more important than any momentary miracle that would have still left me unable to deal with future triggers. As I realised this, it changed my approach to many other things. The things that I often want to happen in a second, instead of taking the time to uproot whatever weeds are in a place, plant good seeds, and wait to see them grow. Because I now know that they surely will.

CHAPTER 12
WE RISE

f I could turn time back to one event, it would be to talk to my father the day he showed up at my house after I got married. That was the last time I ever saw him alive, and for years I held it against him, the grudge of what he had done to our family.

One day, in my late forties, I got a phone call from Barbara and one of my half-sisters.

"Dad died," they said.

On my end of the call, I thought to myself, *Is this is the part where I'm supposed to cry? To be sad?*

I was just numb.

A few years passed after he died, before my sisters and I came together and talked about it. Barbara hadn't been home to Nigeria from the UK in a long time, so it had been a while since all three of us were together in the same place. This was before my fiftieth birthday. We were middle-aged women, yet it was the first time we openly talked about the effects of his actions on us. As my sisters spoke, I realised I hadn't even known how devastated they were. I never knew Gloria and Barbara suffered the consequences of his abandonment just as deeply as I did, until we all gathered years later for a prayer of agreement and let it go.

That day, we prayed for the repose of his soul. There was so much loose emotion in the house, and it made me wonder how we had each survived the years that followed his leaving, hurting as we clearly had been.

We needed to heal.

Unlearning and relearning; for the first time since I became ill in 2009, I understood that getting well is going to be a process that I needed to be patient with. However, committing to an action plan combining medications and therapy had me on my way there. It was a journey, and sometimes results would catch me by surprise.

I just seamlessly transitioned from the person who was scared stiff of socialising to someone who just started living again. One day, I said to myself, *okay, it's time to review my beauty regime; it's time to work on that face and these annoying hyper pigmentation.* I visited B Natural, Ikeja, where a visiting dermatologist from the US was on duty. The dermatologist immediately went to work with laser treatments and expensive bio-restorative facials. These treatments spanned weeks, and gradually, I began to see changes. I also became a regular at Venivici spa for hydrotherapy. I embraced a more deliberate fitness program at the gym, working out three times a week and going swimming in between. Occasionally, Soni and I would take a walk on the Ikoyi Bridge. Then, I decided to join 'team natural' as I stopped applying chemicals to my hair. To boost my wellbeing further, I went back to the wellness spa in Kettering, England; I stayed there one week for a complete detox. As my health improved, I also realised that there were five habits I needed to stick with. I had to learn to manage my stress; I had to find a safe haven; I had to be more purposeful with my spirituality and find time for meditation; I had to own and control my thoughts; and finally, I had to start eating healthier meals and exercising. Perspective counts.

Gradually but steadily, I realised I had entered another season of my life. Spring had sprung. What had felt like winter years—of cold and darkness and withering—were finally passing away and I was regaining my zeal for life; returning to enjoying the things I loved. It felt like a fresh canvas, a chance to write a new vision and dream new dreams. One day, I looked in the mirror and I didn't flinch. I was now looking at life from a fresher perspective.

"I don't know how to be sixty, I only know how to be Betty," I found myself saying often. March 25, 2017 was a good day; it was the day I turned sixty, and I felt as if I had been given a second chance at life. I planned to make the best of it. It had been a whole week of celebration, starting with a surprise birthday party by the G-team, and a nice boat cruise organised by my *aburo*, Bola Balogun, with some of my other *aburos*. Then, there were tea parties here and there. And, I got a chance to grace the cover of *Genevieve* in a sensational Tojufoyeh dress with full blown roses and petals, photographed by Ty Bello. On the cover, I had attempted to share a little insight on depression, making sure to save most of the story for my book; it was a 'Betty' moment for me!

The Birthday celebration itself was a 70s themed disco party deliberately kept small for that intimate fun as it was on my fiftieth birthday. DJ Jimmy Jatt kindly offered his services, and it was so hilarious to see people being seventies-theme compliant. It was such a huge come back as I allowed myself to be silly in my afro and bling bell bottoms, channelling my old school, into an evening of sheer aplomb. Mum was the Glam Ma'am of the evening in her shimmering dress and afro. Soni, Ruyi, and Sonia, were deliriously happy, and altogether, it was a memorable night.

Many people had often wondered how I had stayed looking anything but sixty, I would often pause to find an answer. For me, I do not understand the term 'aging.' Somewhere in my brain, I am unable to process all the talk about aging. I'd like to say I am growing older with each year instead of saying I am aging. I don't know how to be anything but young and youthful. I am not defined by the calendar of my years. I guess I am trapped somewhere between my twenties and my forties. I never think 'aging,' I think 'living and making each day, year and moment count.' That, however, is not to say that I have stayed this way without any effort or discipline. It takes a deliberate wellness regimen to stay fabulous in any age.

People have also asked me if I would indulge in cosmetic surgery, and I always say, "Nothing invasive for me. I wouldn't go under the knife, but anything else is okay by me." In terms of my fashion, I dress to please me; I am not a trend setter. I dress my style in colours. I am not embarrassed to wear pink, floral and appear girly, because deep inside, I will always be that young girl.

Depression was well and truly behind me, and I had returned to wholesome living. Yet, in all of that, I had learnt that as long as I was alive, I could be and do. I couldn't let age or circumstances define me and so, just as I had taken a leap at forty-six to start a magazine, I asked myself, "Betty, what do you want to do with your new lease on life?"

I remembered the day my driver had driven me from Yaba Neuropsychiatric Hospital through the streets of my childhood, and I suddenly knew what I wanted to do. I wanted to tell my story, to put to words the darkest time of my life, and also the joy and strength that followed it. I wanted to use words to paint pictures for everyone else, like I've always done, to let everyone know that the hand of trauma can be broken.

CHAPTER 13
LIFE LESSONS

S peaking up is one of life's most courageous actions; opening up about the misfortunes of our lives sometimes leaves us feeling naked and vulnerable, especially when everyone thinks we have the 'perfect' life. It doesn't help when we are public figures. Unfortunately, many have not come to realise how liberating and therapeutic it is to speak out.

When I launched "Life Lessons with Betty" in February 2017, I realised there were many people – men, women and children – going through things that they would rather not speak about, yet they were grateful I was sharing my own battles. Society makes you feel guilty about things you have no control over; how can anyone blame you for a mental health challenge that brought you to your knees and left you floating like a raft cast away at sea? Speaking about the vicissitudes of my life is one of the bravest things I have had to do.

Here are other lessons I learnt along the way:

- **UNLEARNING**
Unlearning many things I had learnt over the years, was my first lesson learnt from this experience. Inherent cultural beliefs

and habits can enslave us. To break free, to be able to fully live, I had to take my life apart then put each piece back together again. I threw out parts that did not belong to the whole, parts that had no business being there in the first place. I needed to make peace with who I was: the woman in the mirror who wasn't perfect. I told myself some truths, 'What I am going through is a phase and I have the power to change my situation by not revelling in it.' 'I have to fight to get my life back.'

• RELIGION AND DEPRESSION.

'Believe that you're healed and you're healed,' 'It's a satanic attack that calls for deliverance and not therapy or anti-depressants.' These statements are hogwash. Depression and other mental health challenges require professional attention and therapy. Seek help. I have no problems with prayers. There will be days you feel like God has abandoned you, but in the end, you will understand that GOD DOESN'T LOSE BATTLES.

There is a place for logic, there is a place for science, and there is a place for everything God has allowed to be invented. I have a problem with pastors who try to substitute therapy with prayers; pastors who try to convince their congregation that mental health is a spiritual affliction that requires spiritual deliverance. In my search for answers I never allowed myself to fall into that trap. I have heard of some pastors whose children are going through mental health challenges but refuse to let them seek help because "Children of God can't be depressed."

• FIND REASONS TO LIVE.

Suicide always seems like the best solution at the precipice of all the depression. Stop. Take a step back. If there is only just that minuscule flicker of light – of the positive – you can see, grab unto it. Your pain is valid, and you are not alone. Depression is real, you are not going crazy. Depression charades all the negativity in life as the only thing that matters, and brings it all together as one single force against you. It is a kind of darkness that overwhelms the light of life. Find the light, it is always there just beyond the fog of darkness.

As in my own experience, I believe there always remains some parts of us that want to be saved. Do we really want to die or do we want to stop hurting? We might reach a brink where suicide seems the only option, but still in our minds, remains hope that someone or something would be strong enough to bring us back. Hold on desperately to that part. Hold unto that hope. It may seem minute next to the mountain that is depression, yet it is our greatest weapon against it. Hold on to that hope. Let it lead you away from the brink.

The pull is to focus on all the bad, all at once. An alternate option could be to reflect deeper. It is never easy. It is easier said out of the situation, but when you're at your weakest, how do you find the strength to be rational? Slowly. Surely. One step at a time. Are you facing a situation with overwhelming consequences – perhaps bullying or jail time? Can you consider that the situation may change, or that it may become more bearable with time? Are the voices in your head convincing you that life is not worth living or you don't deserve good things? Can you consider that the voices may be wrong? Can you talk back to the voices? Maybe the voices could stop, or change what they tell you, or become less believable with time. Most times, we have an accuser in our minds, but never a defender. Can you try to defend yourself against self-condemning thoughts?

What were your reasons for living before? What has kept you this far? Please, reflect. What have you lived for in the past? Is it possible that you will want to live for those same things again in the future? What was your hope for the future? Remember that depression clouds thoughts, makes hope seem invisible, but it is still there.

- **FIGHT YOUR FEARS.**
If you don't fight, fear *will* cripple you. Don't overanalyse your current state. Fight to remember that the situation is temporary. You will need to dig deep for the strength to fight, and sometimes, you will need to reach out to others for more strength.

- **YOU GET WHAT YOU WORK FOR, NOT WHAT YOU WISH FOR.**
I realised I was only going to get better if I put in work rather than merely wish to get better. That was when I began to actually fight depression. I wanted to get out of the dark tunnel, so I worked at it, with medical help, a positive state of mind, and with affirmations. Then, I got on my feet, and took it one day at a time.

- **DON'T STOKE THE WRONG FIRE.**

I paid undue attention to how I was feeling. I spoke about my emotions and fanned the fire of negativity. I needed to fire up positive energy. I started to consciously control the urge to self-deprecate. I learnt to say, 'When I get better,' instead of 'if I get better.' We need to become more conscious that thoughts become things. Every time I had suicidal thoughts, I neutralised them by thinking of the many reasons why I should live. I would talk back at my depression by affirming that I was getting out of this alive. Every time a negative thought crept up, I would scream, 'NO!' Add, 'I am fine, I am getting better. Enough is enough.' I controlled my thoughts because I realised I owned them, and I was no longer going to allow what I could control to own me. Every time the negative thoughts came up, I neutralised them with joy in my heart.

- **BE GENTLE WITH THE PROCESS.**

I wanted to get out of the twilight zone so fast that I began to fight with what I didn't understand. The more I struggled the more the quicksand engulfed me. I had to stop and understand what was going on with me and tried to understand the process of getting out alive. I learnt to be gentle with myself through the process.

- **SPEAK UP. SPEAK OUT. ASK FOR HELP.**

Don't succumb to the stigma that surrounds depression. *Don't let anyone know you're depressed or you may be labelled mad or crazy and your sanity will be questioned.* We are all suffering from one thing or the other. Speak up and let people help you. A problem shared is often a problem half solved. Let people help you pull through. You *don't* have to go it alone!

- **TRAVEL LIGHT.**

Let go and forgive but never forget the lessons. Through life's travels, you will find that there is no point going about with excess baggage you could easily offload. You will get to your destination faster, lighter.

- **GET BUSY.**

Your down time is a good time to activate your hobbies. Gardening, baking, singing, writing, voluntary charity, designing, teaching? Find your passion. Get out of bed.

- **IT BEGINS IN THE GUTS.**

Detox and cleansing are very crucial to the healing process. What you are eating may be eating you up. Good nutrition and exercise must be factored into quicker recovery. Keep fit. Wellness and wellbeing count. Exercise!

- **DON'T SELF-MEDICATE.**

It might seem ridiculous, but we should all visit a licensed doctor even when we have a cold. Sometimes though, this goes beyond taking antibiotics for a stomach ache. There is a self-medication theory that says people use alcohol and prescribed or over-the-counter drugs, or the effects of other addictive behaviours like eating or gambling, to compensate for underlying social, health or psychological problems that have not been properly treated. These hidden unresolved issues get disguised, and is often belittled by the more visible symptoms. They worsen, then blow up into something that seems beyond cure. The side effects of self-medication can create problems in the future, bigger than what you had first hoped to solve. See a professional.

- **LEARN TO DANCE IN THE RAIN.**

There will be more clouds than sun, still avoid negative zones. Surround yourself with those who do not judge you, people with whom you do not need to continually justify why it's not that easy to 'Power Up' and live a normal life. Surround yourself with love and a lot of positive energy.

EPILOGUE

In Soni's words, "No one ever graduates from this university called 'Life.'" Graduation only takes place in the afterlife, in the presence of the heavenly hosts, if you are lucky. I realised that one of the reasons my sojourn in the wilderness lasted so long was because, unwittingly, I focused too much on what I was going through. I paid homage to it, I revelled in it and didn't fight hard enough. I just rolled with the punches. Medication helped me to get to the place where I realised this and started to fight it. But, this is not the time for 'could haves' or 'should haves,' it is the time to simply chalk everything down to life lessons.

The real tragedy would be if lessons were not learnt, and every mess didn't turn out to be a message of some sort, to ensure other people do not fall into the same trap of paying homage to the down times. 'Power Up,' 'Pull yourself together,' these admonitions may sound insensitive and inappropriate to anyone going through this tunnel of mental health, but when we find the tools to help us— whether medication or therapy—it becomes easier to indeed take charge.

It's amazing how much faster we heal when we begin to control our thoughts instead of allowing them to control us. We must avoid the temptation of magnifying our problems, overthinking and over analysing the 'what ifs.' Life is tough, but if only we knew how much tougher we are with the right mind-set and a spirit that refuses to stay down when life dishes out the total knockouts.

My story is not an invitation to a pity party, so don't go there. It is also not a guide to 'curing' depression because no such thing exists. It is a record of my journey highlighting the trials and triumphs mostly as a guide to others who may be going through the same situation. I am not currently off all my meds either, but I no longer have those bouts of depression. I have been out for over two years now. As for medications, I have graduated from taking 20mg of Nitrazepan to 10mg, and now to 5mg. Eventually, I will totally be rid of it.

Sometimes I forget to take the medication, yet I fall asleep. But then I wake up in the night in panic of not having taken the drugs. I don't wake up because of insomnia, but anxiety and worry that I was doing something wrong. This is a good sign of recovery. I am a long way from the dark days that I hope never to return to. I sometimes have bad days but I am way better than where I used to be.

What has changed is that each day I fight to avoid every trigger. Unlike some time ago, I no longer give in easily to my emotions. I am not a victim; I am a champ. Only champs live to share these kinds of stories. An ugly hot mess now becomes a message of hope to others. It's good to be back on top again!

Here's to everyone who is not giving up without a fight.

AFTERWORD

Six years into our marriage, when Betty was heavily pregnant with our second child, I had my first ulcer attack. I did not know what was wrong with me. I felt a burning sensation in my abdomen. Years of Spartan eating, taking brandy on an empty stomach, and general nonchalance about my health, had finally caught up with me. I was down on my hands and knees, crawling in whatever direction might provide temporary relief from the pain I felt.

I was not used to feeling helpless. I pride myself on being self-reliant and capable of dealing with any issues that life throws my way. At the time, I worked at Radio Nigeria as News Reader and Programme Presenter, and my career as a journalist had taken off, making me a household name around the country. Yet here I was unable to get myself up from the ground and to the hospital to get help. I made a few phone calls to friends and colleagues, but none of them was able to provide any immediate help or relief. I had to get to the hospital, but I was in no position to drive.

And there she was, my wife, nine months pregnant and with a belly that protruded visibly. We met years earlier and married in a modest ceremony. In this state, as the only person able to offer any assistance, I balked at the prospect of her driving. I was in pain, but

I was also nervous. But, she wasn't. She remained calm. "I will drive," she insisted. "We need to get you help."

She got me into the Volkswagen Beetle which she drove at the time, and sat at the wheel. This was a woman just a few days to delivery. In a few hours, we were in the hospital where I was attended to and got relief. Five days later, we welcomed our child.

The event was necessary to illustrate the pragmatic and ultimately dependable nature of my wife from the time we met, dated, and got married—a marriage that has lasted for thirty-five years. She is methodical and analytical. She knew what was important, and could make her case for why it was so. She was never one to feel sorry for herself. But when depression came, it tested us to a point we wouldn't have earlier anticipated.

On one fateful day, we had an argument about some mundane issue that really didn't concern either of us, but it left us each, stubbornly holding on to our side of the argument as we drifted into sleep. The following morning, I said, "Good morning," when I woke up to see her staring at the ceiling. She didn't answer.

"Are you okay?" I asked. After a long pause, when I didn't get an answer from her, I went close to her and said "If it's about the argu..."

I heard her mutter... "I didn't sleep a wink throughout the night."

"So sorry dear.... it was just an argument..."

"I have not been sleeping for some time." Then, I saw tears roll down her eyes. I knew it was serious.

I didn't know much about depression—insomnia I was a little familiar with. Like most Nigerian husbands, I assumed that it was something that came whenever one was upset about something, not something that was debilitating enough to be life threatening, or sustained enough to last over several years. But when it came, first from little benign signs and eventually to a full blown crisis, I did not know how to deal with it.

There were moments when I wondered when this sleeplessness started. Was it after she had our first baby? Was it when she had bouts of malaria attacks that never seemed to stop? Many questions reeled out of my mind trying to make sense of the whole episodes. We had known each other through thick and thin, Betty and I. We are best friends. We also had an anchor in our Catholic faith; it had helped us through countless situations in the past. So I was at a loss as to why we were now in a state where we went from doctor to doctor without finding a lasting solution. The period would defy much of the assumptions I have about managing a health crisis.

At some point, I realised that I was not handling the matter well. Was I showing how worried or doubtful I had become? Was I showing enough compassion? This whole thing was beginning to affect our relationship. She was becoming more irritable and somewhat distant, wanting to be left alone. I feared the worst those times she wanted to be left alone. I would pretend to leave her alone but would just be lurking around. On a few occasions, she would go into the toilet. After a while, I would go near the toilet door and shout, "Betty! Are you okay?" I would feel some relief when I hear her say, "Yeah, I'm fine."

I remember observing Betty on some occasions when, during appointments with doctors, she asked pointed questions that I thought, at the time, were unnecessary. She wanted to know what each drug did, how they worked, the doctor's trust in their efficacy, among other things. She would prove to have been right in the end, as those questions may have saved her life. She trusted, but verified. As exasperating as it may have been sometimes, I realize now that it was a prudent response to an unknown situation, and it probably saved her life. I also started to do some research myself. WebMD, the online medical encyclopaedia, became my go-to place for relevant knowledge on depression and mental illness. Going through this together gave us more of a reason to believe in each other, and grow as a couple.

Betty is blunt. When she's happy, you can tell. You see her become happy-go-lucky. And when she's upset, you knew right there. I thought I had her all figured out, but depression showed us, both of us, that being personally competent, or strong, or analytical, or pragmatic, didn't always help when one is completely overcome with helplessness and despair. Also, because it started not as a long stretch, but pockets and bouts, it was a little hard to understand. As a spouse of someone suffering from depression, it is easy to assume that we know what is going on, or what the solution is. This is not always the case. In my case, there were things I thought I knew, episodes I experienced in a totally different way, which I recently learnt were not what I thought they were, after reading my wife's account written in this book. That is how bad it can sometimes get.

But in all, I am glad to have been with Betty through this journey, and I wouldn't change anything if I had to do it again. I am also hopeful that reading this will help you the reader who may be going through similar ordeals, either as the person to whom it is happening or the spouse. It will be tough, and it will test you to extreme lengths. But if you're tempted to think of how hard it is on you, the spouse, to be there for your partner, think of how hard it is for *them*. This, I think, is the most important way to think about our role. Depression is real, and it happens to people regardless of their class, gender, or place in society. It is also not a death sentence, but it is a burden more easily borne when surrounded by people who care.

Did I always play the cool compassionate guy? No, it was not always easy. There were times I was very angry, wondering why me? Why not any other person? Then I would hear a tiny voice asking "What if it were worse?" I would immediately jump out of such 'defeatist' thought and pray instead. I believe in the power of sincere prayer. Other times, I am busy worrying and wondering how she is feeling only for me to hear her ask, "Soni, are you okay? Have you had a meal?" Then, with relief, I would just smile and say, "I'm cool."

I am glad and thankful to God that it did not get worse than this and that Betty was always willing to find a solution to what I did not know could have been a major threat to our lives and our relationship. We tried to shield our children from our worst fears but they were so great in discerning and treating it with maturity and wisdom as they grew older and became more aware. But in everything, I am glad to have had the privilege of travelling on this journey with someone who completes me in every way.

Soni Irabor (Veteran Journalist)
June 2018
Lagos

ACKNOWLEDGEMENT

Over the years, I have perfected the art of second-guessing myself. I would eagerly embark on a project and then begin to overanalyse why it won't work. All the 'what ifs' would come out to play, the thief called 'procrastination' would rear its head, and the 'great' idea would remain a stillbirth. Not so on this particular book project, I had too many cheerleaders urging me on: "You owe the world a story. Your story deserves to be heard," Linda Ikeji would say. While others would say to me, "It won't be fair if you don't leave the world with a book chronicling your journey... your discovery of who you are... what it took to become the strong personality everyone loves to call 'Aunty Betty,'"

I once thought people were born strong. It wasn't what I could aspire to become until several decades of events in my life reminded me that I couldn't have survived to tell my story if I wasn't strong. It takes a strong woman to defy all odds – stigma inclusive – to open up on her vulnerable trajectory through life. Vulnerability is not a sign of weakness; only the strong can afford to be vulnerable, can afford to share some of the most intimate passages of their lives. I choose to be vulnerable in this way, knowing how many people will be driven to find closure in life, knowing that no matter how long and dreary the tunnel may be, it does lead to a brighter new horizon where hope awaits.

Special kudos to Gbemi Shasore for giving me the necessary motivation to birth this book... and to the Quramo Publishing team, thank you for keeping faith.

Soni, my husband, has been a steadfast partner through the changing scenes of my life. He is my all-season's friend who believes I am this superhero who doesn't know her own strength... "Do you know who you are?" He would ask me on those days life knocked me down. "You are Betty Irabor!" He would remind me, and I would smile. I wish I believed in him as much as he did me.

Omoruyi and Sonia, thank you for being such amazing children. You have both been an integral part of this story I am telling. You never fail to remind me what an inspiration I am, feeding me with my own quotes until I 'power up' again, "...mum, are you not the one who always says, 'whenever you wake up is your morning?' Didn't you teach us to 'do it afraid'?" When I worried about sacrificing my life for Genevieve with nothing to show for it, you would remind me that I wasn't in it for the money but for the purpose of impacting lives... and on and on. Thank you guys – you are the wind beneath my wings.

To my darling Agbegs Gloria, Barbara and Seyi, and their wonderful partners, Uncle Steve, Toks and Bambi, thank you for being the world's best family.

To Iye – Tabitha Uwa Ero – my mother dearest, your prayers didn't go unanswered. We've come a long way because your love for us kept us going on days when we would have crumpled like rags. Uwese Iye!

To my friend, Barbara Lawrence, thank you for showing me what true friendship is, and for always being just a phone call away.

A special thank you to Kola Tunbosun and Kadaria Ahmed, for going the extra mile to ensure that Dust to Dew has that extra flavour.

My dear personal assistant, Osas Omigie, thank you for the long days we worked and reworked the manuscript to meet the deadline.

To my Genevieve team since 2003... here's to you guys.

Dear God... thank you for not giving up on me when I gave up on you and on myself. You were always there to still the storm. I wasn't consumed because mercy said NO!

To all who have always believed in me, even when I couldn't see the forest for the trees, thank you. Accolades to Y'all!

Finally, I leave you with my favourite hymn of all times, 'Morning has broken'...

Morning has broken like the first morning
Blackbird has spoken like the first bird
Praise for the singing
Praise for the morning

Praise for them springing fresh from the worlds
Sweet the rain's new fall, sunlit from heaven
Like the first dewfall on the first grass
Praise for the sweetness of the wet garden
Sprung in completeness where his feet pass
Mine is the sunlight
Mine is the morning
Born of the one light Eden saw play
Praise with elation, praise ev'ry morning
God's recreation of the new day

ABOUT THE AUTHOR

Betty Irabor has been a major player in the Nigerian publishing industry for over fifteen years. She is the editor-in-chief/CEO of Nigeria's leading lifestyle magazine, 'Genevieve.' Widely celebrated on global platforms, she has been featured on 'The Entrepreneurial Edge' on CNBC, Forbes Woman Africa's 'Against all Odds,' and BBC's 'The Conversation.' She was the Creative Curator of the Cointreau creative crew for its 'Dream, Dare, Create' campaign which was aimed at developing women's freedom and expression. She also sat on the board of Total Nigeria Ltd. as a jury member in the STARTUPPER project for young entrepreneurs.

She is the founder of the 'Pink Ball Foundation' which initiated the conversation on breast cancer awareness in Nigeria. Her first book, "Morning Dew," was a clarion call for women to live a purposeful life. She was named a Hero for the Lancôme Paris 'My Shade. My Power' beauty campaign in Nigeria. She is also a recipient of several awards. Betty Irabor is passionate about reaching out to the younger generation of women and sharing her wealth of experience. She is known for her strong influence in impacting and influencing thoughts; she steadily shares her story at the risk of being vulnerable, in order to encourage others to succeed against all odds.

Betty Irabor is a wife and a mother with a very supportive family.